AGE OF
Autonomy

Harry Colcord

Table of Contents

Preface

The history of economic performances evidence successes and failures in various forms. Self-sustaining individual based work routines advanced to command/control based companies. The development of nations has been directly related to enhancements in management. With the help of W. Edwards Deming, Japan may be the best example in history of how management quickly advanced the economy of a nation. The harnessing of human energy in systemic measurable performance has created tremendous results for mankind. With the ubiquitous nature of knowledge and the tools of management, it is just as likely that the orderly destruction of most if not all management structure will provide mankind with advances in living standards that are equally as positive. It would be silly to suggest that organizations will suddenly disappear. In many instances, the organized efforts needed to harmonize individual acts into collective output will continue to mandate organizations. It is also likely that what we still term unemployment will soon be seen as non-employment as functions disappear forever, with tasks increasingly absorbed by ever more effective tools and people.

What follows has been written for my sons, Jason, Jared and Harrison. It started as a journal, a checklist of items that I had hoped my sons could use if ever needed. As I wrote about business functions and the people I have met, the story and my opinions grew into this short book. If no one else ever reads what follows, I am hoping my experience, educations and perspectives have some value in some way for one or all three sons. If I ramble and meander beyond what might normally be acceptable, it is likely because I simply chose to write, edit and lay out things myself. As a possible tool for my sons, I want this to be from me, not simply paid for by me. The single exception is to thank Theresa Diers, my partner, for hours of typing my handwritten notes.

Interspersed herein are my thoughts about business, knowledge and a suggested progression toward autonomy. This progression should include the creation of many new tools which free, teach and amalgamate talent toward the enhanced production of goods and services deemed to be of value in various markets. A terrific possible result in the return toward autonomous producers may be an advance in the dignity of man, interdependent but clearly more self-reliant.

In the Influencer section, because I have been fortunate to have been affected by a number of business leaders, I have reviewed and commented on the impressions I developed when I was exposed to each of them.

I am not an experienced writer; rather, I have been a practitioner who has spent a career with constant curiosity about how management works. I have tried to acknowledge Peter Drucker's work which should be obvious throughout. Generally, Dr. Drucker supplied us with the best questions and we, as practitioners, tried to fill in the blanks. In my listing of strategic questions and objective categories, I have used Drucker's lists as the starting points. If you find yourself in business and questioning your approach or next steps, read Drucker first, his questions will likely lead you to the best answers. What follows are more opinions than facts.

Age of Autonomy

Yankee ingenuity is the reference to early settlers and the
need to use what was available in a flexible, adaptable manner.
Immigrants who arrived in areas of New England expected to
find readily plant worthy land but found conditions far different
than they expected. Nonetheless, they worked with the land and
used materials they found and did what they needed to do to
survive. Ingenuity can be viewed in the history of most rugged
places where people find themselves challenged with the need to
survive and prosper.

Business ingenuity has not been exclusive to America, but,
it has been strong for 150 years. In the cycle that has seen
us fragment labor into effective processes, we have led the
world in the innovation and production of most products
used throughout the industrial era of our existence. It is
interesting that continuous improvements in processes and
technology have likely led us full circle. The autonomy of the
immigrant who found challenging circumstances yet, cleared
land, built shelters, planted and harvested crop and stored
and sold his excess was phase one. The fragmenting of labor,
the growth of interdependence, the creation of management
and management functions was phase two. Now, in migratory
rather than revolutionary fashion, the decentralization of labor

and knowledge, the "creative destruction" of functions and the creative construction of a new autonomy should foster a new age.

It is likely that the greatest reward in this new age of autonomy will not be material; rather, it will be psychological. When we look back at the effects fractionalized labor had on the satisfaction felt by workers, history has abundant examples of unhappy workers wanting more than a wage, piece work or a punch clock. While it would be a stretch to suggest that the producers in the Age of Autonomy will be self-actualized in the classic sense described by Abraham Maslow, the control inherent in autonomy should provide a very satisfying sense of independence for those who employ Yankee ingenuity successfully.

It is beyond me to predict how autonomous talent will be amalgamated in the Age of Autonomy. It surely provides innovation opportunities for those capable of identifying talent and expertise and able to segment talent so that it can be orchestrated in an effective operating model. Specialization, operation, education and the creation of new tools for every existing function is likely an enormous opportunity for creative people in this latest, new frontier.

Some discussion of history seems reasonable. Somewhere, a very long time ago, someone exchanged something with someone for something different. The exchange or barter was likely very simple, the quid pro quo of "this for that" was likely just an exchange accompanied by a grunt of approval without any conflict. Comparison of material cost and value added had not yet occurred. If a stick was traded for a rock, perceived value likely allowed the exchange to occur without violence or bloodshed.

Then, the guy with the stick took his stick home and the guy with the rock, also headed home. A wife looked at the stick, old and fragile, and laughed at the shellacking her man had taken in the trade. At the same time, the other wife applauded her man's skill in having traded the fragile stick for the solid rock. Here, we have something akin to an early example of a business transaction and marital exchange!

There was no currency, no formal production, no competition, just a perception of value and a subsequent trade. From that early transaction, whatever it was, we have evolved into a rather complex world. Values, services, products and currency have continuously changed. Currency will likely soon have no basis in any economy. That will change a number of economic factors on its own, especially related to tracking and taxes, but, that is another story.

If these first traders were here today, they would likely be stunned by the evolution of business functions. Marketing, research, engineering, sales, operations, controls, systems, finance, etc., have grown into complex organs combining to produce a very complex organization. Grasping appropriate priorities within such a complex organization is mindboggling for any but the most intimately involved and highly trained individual.

Could it be that we have simply gone too far? Long ago Dr. Peter Drucker pointed out that opportunity only exists outside the business. Everything that exists inside the business is cost. In structure, similarly, everything outside the business relates to market and everything inside the business relates to data. Predictably, functions, whether old or new are built into complex organs with tentacles that typically weave throughout the business. They build their own languages, their own associations and their own leadership, often insulated from each other and even from the customer. Drucker tried to get us to distinguish between the need for activity versus the need for function. It is more often than not likely that we succumb to the desire to add function because inherently, functional designations add more prestige than simply accomplishing that which is effectively accomplished with completing tasks. To say that I am the head of Research and Design is more impressive than to say that I have considered and shown new ways to make our products or services more valuable to our customers.

Labor in its earliest form was a comprehensive set of tasks which produced a complete product. The farmer prepared the land, planted the seed and harvested the crop. The blacksmith sourced material, heated the metal, pounded and shaped it and sold and collected for his product.

An early observation of the value of a "division of labour" came from Adam Smith in Wealth of Nations, 1776. Smith suggested that by dividing labor, that is, by specializing tasks, a pin factory might produce thousands of pins a day. By comparison, a single man, completing all of the required tasks might only be capable of producing a few pins a day. Even Adam Smith would likely be surprised by the advances in effectiveness in pin production. In his era, a factory could produce 5000 pins a day with specialized functions. By the mid-19th Century, a factory could produce 70,000 pins a day. Today, online, one can buy a pin making machine for $5000 which produces 5,000,000 pins a day. Suffice it to say, labor has changed.

While productivity was greatly enhanced through separating tasks, separation likely ended the sense of dignity that a craftsman or farmer derived from completing all tasks, from being his own business. There would seem to be a sense of compromise that the craftsmen needed to accommodate when the security of gain from greater productivity through interdependent labor replaced the independence of self-reliant work which produced complete products. Imagine if you will the move from being whole to simply becoming part. Abraham Maslow, referring to his famous "Hierarchy of Needs" might have suggested that the craftsmen who completed all tasks could feel "self-actualized" on Maslow's pyramid. The laborer who succeeded him might feel his survival and sustenance needs were met but, dignity was likely lost through the loss of independence. The gains in productivity were indisputable.

However, Adam Smith did not discuss the possible adverse effects that dividing labor would cause in the dignity of man. While slow, the worker who completed all of the tasks required to produce the pin was whole. The worker who became a cog in the wheel of production became interdependent and controlled. The concept of the individual as a whole entity versus the individual who completes limited tasks within an entity is critical for understanding the opportunity we now enjoy with changing technology and a slow return to the autonomous producer.

Historically, continuing improvement in the use of labor occurred in the 19th century. Eli Whitney is credited with various innovations in using labor in a "repeatable" manner. Mid-19th century, Chicago meat packers began using pulley systems that allowed workers to complete butcher tasks from fixed positions as meat passed by them.

Late in the 19th century, Frederick W. Taylor is credited with the first in depth study of the performance of labor. In a number of references, Peter Drucker refers to Taylor as the pioneer who first decided that labor deserved a system of observation. Taylor's 1911, "The Principles of Scientific Management" moved work to an organized level. While Taylor is credited with the first detailed study of work through recording and analyzing "time and motion," he also set key principles for human resource management. In addition to the study of tasks, Taylor asserted the need to train and develop employees, to supervise workers and to specifically divide the tasks of managers and workers. While effective in improving productivity, the focus on the detailed performance of labor did provoke workers and caused numerous labor strikes at the time.

At the same time Taylor was publishing his treatise, the Ford Motor Company was developing its famous assembly line between 1908 and 1915. In an interrelated set of events, Ford dramatically changed transportation, society and the very nature of work.

Ford did not create the automobile or the assembly line. Ford was influenced by the meat packing lines in Chicago and motivated by the desire to put the automobile within the financial reach of most Americans. What Ford did do was remake the process of assembly so that men became fixed and parts moved to and from them. In a simple observation, Ford Motor Company turned man into machine! The consequences were staggering. Cars became available at ever decreasing prices. They were no longer reserved for the rich. People once again began to move, to explore, to shop. The implications for change within a moving society had a profound effect. A simple example was that the Sears catalog was no longer the sole source for many products; women could now go shopping. Sears General Robert Wood saw the light and began an era of store building and incredible success.

The price paid by the worker seems to have been the loss of dignity that comes from being such a small part of the whole. While Henry Ford pointed to steady wages, expanded purchasing power and a general advance of lifestyle, workers hit obvious discontent. Production soared as demand for the moderately priced Model T exploded. However, the employee turnover at Ford reached epoch proportions in 1913, likely causing Ford to gamble on the $5 day. While competitors thought the high wage would ruin the company, it actually created greater demand for the Model T and the sense that Henry Ford was a hero to the worker. While this did forestall growing worker unrest, for our purposes it is simply reviewed as an example of how a change in the way work was accomplished, changed the functions of business and the character of work.

It seems reasonable to repeat, paraphrase and consider Peter Drucker's observation regarding why businesses exist at least a couple thousand times. <u>Business exists to create and retain customers.</u> Certainly, management exists to foster economic performance within business but, management is not needed in any business where the effort to create and retain a customer is not accomplished.

In considering the relevance, reward and retention of any function within a business, the constant audit question should be how the task you perform enhances our ability to create and retain customers. For the 19th century farmer or craftsmen the review was simpler and comprehensive. For the 21st century business, the review is muddled in functional complexity that has gone too far. If we want to see a return to strong economic performance within a business, it seems that evolving toward a more independent worker, joined with all appropriate players required, will give us the best chance to satisfy customer wants and needs.

This is not some Pollyannaish or esoteric view. Rather, it seems to be a practical continuing evolution of Druckers "knowledge worker" in an age where the availability of information continues to grow exponentially and the willingness and ability to commit to employment decreases consistently. It is becoming the Age of Autonomy!

In my simple experience, an example of function versus activity occurred with the systems group which provided service to the group of manufacturing companies for which I had responsibility. At the time, in the mid 1980's, large platforms from companies like IBM and Digital Equipment Corporation (D.E.C) were used to provide maximum computing capabilities on a shared machine, too large and expensive to be purchased by any individual company within the group. Services were requested by each company and then considered and scheduled by the systems function leadership. Slowly, but surely, the backlog of systems work grew to six months. Now, keep in mind that the system people were good people. The problem was that the complexity of the function designation removed systems workers from appreciating the nature of the businesses they served and the actions that were warranted. So, after reasonable review and discussion, we fired all systems associates and suggested they reapply at each and or all of the companies within our group. One master technician was retained to manage the machine and most other systems associates went on to operate the systems activities within the individual companies, much closer to the action, much closer to the needs of customers.

While the above example is very old, the relevance is current. Had we failed to prioritize the need for action over the sanctity of function, we would likely have also failed to recognize the advent of decentralized systems which obviously overtook centralized computing. The players would surely have banded together to protect turf rather than serve customer needs. Drucker always asked, "What is the task? Why do it at all?"

The framework of business grew dramatically in the 20th century. It is; to borrow a phrase from that century, "time to tear down those walls." I suggest that restructuring begin with the most basic concept, that is that all functions, all tasks, all responsibilities fit in one of two categories, market or data. Market exists to discover and serve customers and non-customers. Data encompasses all costs, including supply, needed to serve markets. Before you decide that your business is different and cannot use such simple framework, I beg you to read on. My biases are well developed and may not in fact work for your business, but, you will have invested very little in the consideration process.

On the subject of business, it is rare for me to disagree with Peter Drucker on any issue. One such rare place occurs on p. 62 of Management, Tasks, and Responsibilities Practices. In discussing Cyrus McCormick, Drucker says, …"he also invented the basic tools of modern marketing, market research and market analysis, the concept of market standing, pricing policies, the service salesman, parts and service supply to the customer, and installment credit." For me, the grouping is conflicting, outside tasks, market tasks are grouped with inside costs, reactive costs which are responsive to perceived market needs. "Pricing policies, the service salesman, parts and service supply to the customer, and installment credit "are costs belonging to data. The do not relate to market, to who is the customer, what is value? They are responsive. Marketing questions ask, what is there, what is needed or wanted, what do we do or what do we make? Data questions ask, what has been or is being done, at what cost, with what result?

Before moving farther, comments about what I consider a basis for thinking are appropriate. The near collapse of the global economy, very much like 1929, caused me to focus on the history of business.

Cycles humble, cycles cleanse. If you read John Kenneth Galbraith's Crash of 29, you will feel like you may be watching the news today. Speculation on real estate in Florida, Charles Ponzi selling lots near a non-existent Florida city at 23 lots to the acre, borrowing massive amounts at favorable rates to buy large amounts on margin all occurred in the 1920's...and again in the first decade of the 21st century.

Businessmen earned such disdain in the early 20th century that healthcare and government managers no longer wanted to be categorized in the profession. As a result, the era saw a change in designation to Public Administration and Health Administration, distinctly separate from Business Administration. With all we endure in crisis, the opportunity, the compelling need to survive creates a great chance to right our wrongs.

The cries of foul aimed at the excesses of executives would be comical if the comedy had not created such horrible results. The comedy seems to be the cheering turned jeering when publicly responsible executives usher us to wealth and then, in what should be predictable cycles, flush all we gained.

For economic performance, which should be clearly differentiated from social well-being, it seems that ideal governance is that which promotes open thinking while in private, but, squelches such things in public. The prospect of a free, unlimited concept of liberty causes creative, productive juices to flow. Coupling that with the fear that overt action will be met with dire consequences can keep the economy focused and productively effective. This seems to be what China has done so well. Almost certainly, as Chinese workers grow more accustomed to survival in a post-agrarian society, their demands for greater freedom will become more and more disruptive and will result in decreased productivity of manual labor. While this may seem all too obvious, the key to sustained long-term economic success may be the creation of a society which self-imposes the restrictions on public freedom which failed so miserably in the era of communism. As China inevitably sees consumables increase from 30% of GDP toward our 70% consumption, we will see how their grand experiment performs.

What is written here is intended to suggest ways to enhance performance in the simple actions that may be appropriate for running a business. The chance to comment on economics and the cyclical crises that affect business is simply a bonus!

The rules that relate to public businesses should be different than the rules related to private businesses. The rationale for this basic perspective is who has taken risk, which deserves reward. On the public side, shareholders, once an offering has been made, are the risk takers. Executives within public companies are entrusted with most of the tasks and responsibilities as their private counterparts. They are however, absent a major risk that private businesses face, the risk of loss of invested capital.

So, someone, somewhere, somehow, should set standards for what is appropriate for public and by all means, leave private, private. Boards of directors for most public companies are a joke. The election of directors should be by shareholders in contests with issues and positions.

In any case, the work related to running businesses is what will be reviewed and challenged herein. Discussion of strategy and the criteria used to set direction will be followed by a review of operating functions and the tools used in management to assess performance.

My experiences, positive and negative influence most of what I suggest as relevant. My studies, especially of Peter Drucker's observations absolutely influence and guide my thinking and approach to the various elements of business thinking. Recognizing that business norms evolve, my comments will relate to functions as they exist, with my own views and biases; along with how functions may change.

The "creative destruction" that is occurring has been and will continue to be very painful for people who see the omission of their functions forever. The obvious extinction has already occurred for many executive and administrative support people. It is almost comical to reflect on how my executive assistant started each day bringing me coffee. There are more comments about expertise and how personalities will be considered and tolerated later. Suffice it to say that the number of people needed to manage the work of other people will continually decline as individuals increasingly become solely responsible for finding and completing work in settings where all contributors function independently, but, in harmony.

Management Conventions

Management Conventions do at least set basic parameters for how decisions are made. Specialization within practices like medicine refine procedures for greater success than the performance of the old line "Doc" accomplished as the only option in the 19th century.

In reverse, we have historically labeled what we have seen. In the 1960's Douglas MacGregor coined Theory X which was the command control label. Theory Y was the interactive, participative label. After MacGregor and Drucker argued for the employment rights of man, Maslow pointed out that many people needed to be controlled in order not to have them operate out of control, ineffective for their own well-being.

Maslow, more so than management theorists, sought to understand the nature of man. As the greatest observer of people in management, Drucker was admittedly a "bystander". People are part and parcel in management but, process, practice and results are the outcomes. For Maslow, behavior, inputs and results were the focus. While Drucker and MacGregor espoused themes, Maslow understood specifics. In reflection, there was a young man in my past who seemed to operate at an extreme unfathomable to me. His anger, violence and lack of remorse were unparalleled in my experience. After he was interviewed by a counselor, we asked the counselor for advice and an opinion. The opinion was that this young man lived "without a conscience." No matter what he chose to do, he had no regret simply because he did not reflect on what he had done. While extreme, imagine giving this young man freedom to operate as he saw fit within a group. If Maslow had built a pyramid suggesting the latitude appropriate for players on any team, it would likely look very similar to his "Hierarchy of Needs" pyramid. Control at the base would involve training and monitoring. Appropriately a progression up the pyramid would be tied to measurable results enumerating experience, skills and scores. At the peak of the pyramid, only the CEO would be "self-actualized" and even he/she would be checked by a board of directors.

For the well-being of society and the equity and bond investor, extremes occur where prisoners remained shackled to a chain gang while CEO's are given performance incentives to build profitable enterprises.

I know almost nothing about breaking wild horses but, I envision the wild horse as a thing of beauty. Unbridled, it rears, wails and runs. To make the wild horse effective as transportation, it was "broken" and trained. The loss of freedom was sad but the transition to transportation was very effective for the greater good.

Within the management of human resources bridling is simply a way to keep controls very well defined until we know the direction and speed our associates will likely move. People like Henry Ford never bought into the concept of unbridling. A classic Theory X practitioner, Ford simply needed doers to do what he thought needed to be done.

Practically, there is nothing wrong with Theory X at the start of a business or in some cases where the business is fighting for survival in exceptional circumstances.

It is fascinating to consider the migration of considerations regarding use of human resources over the past hundred or so years. The farmer or craftsman relied almost entirely on his own skills and the support of family members who assisted him. Then, the blacksmith and the farmer realized increased output through the employment of a helper who did some of his work. Then, work was analyzed, dissected and split into functions as first discussed by Adam Smith more than one hundred years earlier. Through the twentieth century the segmentation of labor, the push for production, the organization and push back by unionized workers, the creation of functional human resource management and the revolutionary explosion of information all took place. So much of what occurred in the twentieth century was evolutionary, responsive and practical.

Then, two thirds of the way through the century, an explosion occurred. The worldwide web created exactly what that name describes, the entire world linked in a web of interactivity that is data and socially intense. The break from an evolutionary process has already happened but has not been fully recognized in management structure and function. All of the concern considered in Theory X and Theory Y thirty years ago resulted in William Ouchi's theory, Theory Z. Theory Z was a more considerate approach where loyalty was supposed to go both ways. Some of this was born in the lifetime employment which Japanese companies committed to in the 1980's. That sense of commitment was combined with the suggestion that continuous cross-training was appropriate for people who would be together forever. It all sounded wonderful at the time but then, so did IBM's no layoff for life policy. Eventually, reality bit Japan and IBM.

If X, Y, and Z no longer hold favor as management conventions, what should be next? I suggest Theory K. Theory K is first a tribute to Dr. Drucker and the volumes he produced on the importance of the knowledge worker for about one-third of his near one hundred year life. Knowledge takes the top slot in criteria for employment. K can also represent approval, especially in the abbreviated world we now communicate. K in transactional analysis relates appropriately to I'm Ok, You're Ok, which is the seminal work of author Thomas A. Harris, M.D. In today's world where knowledge is everywhere for everyone, we should all feel okay about the flattening of availability to one and all.

The beauty of knowledge for all is that capability has expanded exponentially. The compensating ugly side of all-inclusive availability of knowledge is that most specialization by implication no longer has value. In fact, for top management, specialization can only be justified because of an inability or unwillingness to use that which is generally available.

Productivity improvements for the past 50 years have largely been owing to the creation and continuous improvement in processes and technology utilized by specialty players within their various fields of expertise. The next wave of productivity improvements should be possible with the complete elimination of most specialties. Harkening back to Drucker and others, nothing is more wasteful than doing well that which need not be done at all.

Within Theory K, building scores seems to be a good place to start tracking performance. Activities should be scored on a customer required and non-customer required basis. Persistent effort to identify, scrutinize and minimize non-customer activities should be the easiest way to improve performance via cost reductions. We should recognize that there will likely be a change in how people are viewed within the general availability and distribution of knowledge.

As so much has improved in volume, quality, availability and speed of information flow, there seems to have also been a change in sentiment regarding people. Expertise was more valuable in the past. What might have been contained in one brain was not readily available to all. Dependence and benefit created an environment where talented individuals could be temperamental, even contrary, without the threat of reprisal. In a different spin on high tech balanced by high touch, the reduction in the value of expertise is likely to be met by the need for team members to be more compassionate in order to be acceptable within the group. It is more likely that mediocre performance will be tolerated when it is coupled with extraordinary attitude. In other words, there will continue to be a premium on positive attitude. Conversely, a bad attitude coupled with strong technical competence will have less value simply because the technical information and skills are more readily available from multiple resources.

Creating new measures of performance should be a valuable human resource task. Criteria that measure the importance of task may be coupled with measures of how an individual personality enhances or detracts from the team's atmosphere and performance.

Vacating traditional business norms will not be an easy task. Structure has been developed, defined and fortified over a 120 year period. If we think about what religion has done over thousands of years of existence, the point here may be better understood but, not necessarily better accepted.

Religions generally start with strong ideals. As structure is added, parameters become better defined and more restrictive. Free thinking is corralled by rules that require conformance by members. Positive change is adversely affected by time spent on buildings, robes and rules. In a similar vein, business structure and the energy needed to create, control and grow structure has detracted from simply focusing on tasks that serve customers.

Surely, the structure that was created in business was generally needed to manage the complex operations that were created last century. But, increasingly, structure becomes the negative enabler in business performance that structure in religion created in spirituality. Not only is creativity squelched, horrible behavior is condoned as befitting beliefs. In business, precious resources are used to manage managers who likely are no longer needed. While it would be naïve to suggest that various forms of negotiations, sales and service are not required, the control needed to monitor and make decisions are now likely mechanical rather than manpower. It seems appropriate to beat an important Druckerism over and over. What is the task? Why do it at all?

The first task for top management in the coming change is strategic. Where appropriate and when appropriately timed, the strategic statement should suggest that "less" structure, "less" organization, "less" functions are required to find and retain customers. The objectives that follow such strategy should define how knowledge as a commodity and technical tools as specialties, combine to provide an even better product or service. Let's look at functions.

CEO

Fundamentally, execute is the little discussed requirement in executive work. While obvious in definition, the implications of execution fail to be considered reasonably. Even Dr. Drucker, the greatest thinker regarding executive work, fails to define executive work completely. Drucker refers to management as the work of the executive. Within management, Drucker discusses leadership and tasks as inherent. If only for clarity sake, defining leadership, operating and management as distinct functions within executive work allows prioritization of the appropriate requirement for the business. In this 21st century, where knowledge workers are better defined as co-workers, rather than associates or subordinates, task distinctions within executive work becomes increasingly more important. You will see within the outline I have used to frame and define priorities for business, the need to decide what is most important at a point in time review, operating skill, leadership or management prowess. The effective organization is that which addresses the tasks required (i.e. work) to meet the customers' expectations, or, at least do better than competition in satisfying the customer.

Effective executive work properly meets the need, albeit always changing, for operating skill, leadership and/or management of people and capital, in the appropriate priority and intensity.

The definition of operating skill, leadership and management will vary with perspective but can always be defined as work. Drucker tells us that for any idea to produce results, it must be reduced to work. So, the definition below relates to work, not vision or strategy.

Having "vision" is great; sharing your vision, selling it, defining it, while delegating responsibility to appropriately chosen champions is the first part of executive work. Developing and using appropriate controls begins to assure performance.

Leadership success relies upon:
- Past successes
- Current vision
- Ability to communicate one or both

Management requires:
- Recruitment and selection of talent
- Understanding work
- Training
- Clearly defining tasks and responsibilities
- Monitoring progress and results
- Recognizing and rewarding performance (motivating-no matter which: the subordinate, associates, co-workers...he/she needs to know when they have had a good day.)

Operating skills require:
- Performing assigned operating activities toward successful completion of tasks.
- Invest, utilize and replace the capital required to complete tasks
- Utilizing experience to accomplish any or all of the above. Experience connects past activities with current optional action. Triggers are thus pulled with confidence even though actual results may vary.

When you consider the position of CEO, the role has contained the psychology of autonomy closest to the individual in a sole proprietorship. Although the CEO relies on the management of others for performance, the position of "King of the Hill" encompasses the whole of the business and is not merely a cog in the wheel.

If we go back to Adam Smith's example of the production of a pin we can appreciate the measure of autonomy the CEO feels compared to other workers. The CEO not only has the basis for garnering respect or engendering fear, he/she also likely has the best chance of equaling or exceeding his/her lot if the enterprise fails and alternate employment is required.

In my experience, the critical tasks of the CEO are setting strategy and selection and retention of talent. While involvement in objective setting is reasonable, authorship and ownership is best fostered at the relevant operating level, where the objective should be set, owned and where the work should occur. While the CEO may be entrusted with the most power in the business, power has more importance by implication than by use. Once used, most of the value of power is gone.

With Peter Drucker's influence in almost every word, I developed the Strategic and Operating checklists below over the 23 years I served as a general manager, group President and finally CEO of the enterprises that employed me:

STRATEGIC PLAN

STRATEGIC THINKING

a).   Threats (from industry, from competition, from
       customers, from suppliers, etc.)
- Opportunities (for industry, from competition)
- What do we do well?
- What do we do poorly?

- What do our competitors do well?
- What do our competitors do poorly?
- What are the peaks?
- What are the valleys?

b).   Develop an initial summary of what we deduce.

GENERAL STRATEGIC QUESTIONS:

- What is our business?
- Who is the customer? Various, the more defined, the better your chances. Include what, where, when, why and how likely is any factor to change?
- What should we:

    a) Abandon

    b) Maintain status quo

    c) Push

- What will our business be?

    a) Remember that it will be different. If you do most things as usual, where will we be in the future?

- What should our business be:

    a) Combine opportunity discussion along with willingness to take risks, and, provide organization and measured feedback.

    b) What more can be sold to current customers? Where can new customers be found? Who are the non-customers?

2A) STRATEGIES (Develop Qualitative statements, more, less, best, etc.)

REVIEW MISSION STATEMENT (DRIVING FORCE) (HISTORY) (WHO WILL WE SERVE)

PEOPLE

- If not already here, would you hire? Remember, this is strategy related to talent, not specific performance reviews.
- Perception of what is needed? More leadership traits, more operating skills or greater management prowess. Are sufficient knowledge and teaching skills present to accomplish?

OPERATIONAL PLAN

1) DESCRIBE THE PROCESS BY WHICH YOU OPERATE: List each function and describe how the baton is passed. List all DISCIPLINES that must be maintained/measured/enhanced to assure continuity in the process. (Whether in a traditional operation or an amalgamation of autonomous workers, this discipline is still important.)

OBJECTIVE SETTING:

A) Explain why something should be done at all.

B) Define what will be done by when, by whom, at what cost and with what benefit.

C) Action steps that are clearly assigned as work.

D) Indicators of success.

E) Follow up dates.

3) SPECIFIC OBJECTIVE AREAS: (Anything without an objective will be ignored…like most of "my ideas," this is yet another Druckerism. I have used the Drucker list of objective categories and added suggestions and definitions which helped me)

Objectives:
- Objectives must be work and must be flexible.
  A) Marketing
    - Concentration concern, market share within market segment, and the theater in which we will fight the war.

      1. Who is the customer?

      2. What is value for them?

      3. How do they buy?

      4. What do they need?

         A) What tools prepare us to sell effectively?

         B) The goal is to "know" so well that selling isn't needed.

  B) Innovation

      1. Innovation related to product or service.

      2. Innovation related to consumer behavior and values.

      3. Innovations in skills needed to bring product and service to market.

C) Human Organization
- Human Resource objectives, for attitudes, and skills needed (training and retaining). Also, recruiting is an "outside market". Distinguish right person issue from right role, right relationship decisions.

D) Financial Resources
- Objective for use of capital (sources, with whom you compete for capital)

E) Physical Resources

   1. Use of space (options)

   2. Development of sources of supply especially (vendors)

F) Productivity measurements (controls)

   1. Pricing, what is too little, too much? Why? Profit is a business cost. Too little and you cannot fund growth. Too much and competition will do whatever is needed to dethrone you.

   2. Human Resources, output in units, dollars and profit per wage dollar invested.

   3. Cost of money and return.

   4. Space/physical sales dollars per square (inch, foot, yard)

G) Social Responsibility

   1. Harmony with the community is important.

H) Profit Requirements

1. The means for investing in objectives and rewarding risk.

<u>NOTE:</u> Objectives must be balanced against: 1) attainable profit, 2) demands of immediate and distant future and 3) each other, with trade-offs (risk decision).

BUDGETING:

A) Management staff reviews recent period performance.

B) History should be reviewed, not relied upon. Each capital and operational dollar should be proposed as an investment in future opportunity. We cannot invest in past performance.

C) Budget premises are written by affected managers, by department, by line.

D) Objectives are assimilated, deducing financial implications.

E) Profit is budgeted as an objective, not a result.

F) Joint management review results in agreement or rework.

<u>NOTES:</u>
- Planning is a process, not an event. Next year begins one short day after this year ends.
- Innovations are excluded from budgets for 2 years.

POTENTIAL REWARDS:
- Objectively tied to results (in advance).

DECISIONS MAKING PROCESS:

A) Level of authority.

B) Procedures for big and small decisions.

CONTROLS NEEDED:

A) Pulse (key daily/weekly indicators).

B) What items should be measured/how often (balance sheet, income statement). Every line listed should be owned by an individual.

C) Unique characteristics?

D) Incidental data should be identified so that it can be ignored.

JOB DESCRIPTIONS:

• Describe simply, starting with the reason the position exists. Ask each manager to list his/her top 5 responsibilities. You do the same, for comparison.

A) List minimum level of acceptable performance.

B) Agree on standards that allow that associate to know if they have a good day.

C) Tell each where our company is going, most do not know.

ORGANIZATION CHART:

A) Functions

B) Chart interrelationships

C) Match with individuals.

HIRING/INTERVIEWING TIPS:

A) Performance Skills-Example:
- Oral Skills
- Organization
- Problem solving

B) Technical Skills are easier to analyze. Performance Skills (i.e. tact, team play, etc.) required discussion of past experiences, behavior and how circumstances were handled.

C) Explain that you <u>will</u> take notes and why.

D) Ask candidate to describe situations by example. How did they act with friends at work, adversaries at work? Past actions are good indicators of future actions.

E) Seek a balanced picture of the candidate.
- Build Rapport
- Ask open ended questions
- Take notes
- Allow for silence
- Maintain control
- Be candid, ask for examples which exemplify weaknesses & strengths
- Take time to evaluate information from interview
- Don't sit back and listen, sit up and listen.

F) Let the best performers in the company establish the seven most important behaviors for the new people. Have them vote until they reduce it to seven or eight.

Note: The above is not suggested as an all-inclusive tool.

The long range success of the CEO and the enterprise rests on disciplined attention to the detailed work needed to create new customers and retain old customers. In reflecting on my own mediocre years as a CEO, I felt reasonably balanced in these required disciplines. I also felt quite comfortable communicating with competitors and even befriending a few over the years. Upon reflection, there was however a fierce sense of frenzy when competition brewed from within the company. In my case and while only conjecture, in the cases of many CEO's: competition from within is akin to the act of a traitor. My sense is that the feeling that one is self-actualized as a CEO is shaken deeply at various levels when CEO's consider the threat of competition. Andrew Grove of Intel wrote a terrific book whose title lends credibility to such a perspective, "Only the Paranoid Survive." When asked what Apple might look like 5 years after Steve Jobs death, I suggested they will be average, frenzy at the extreme likely died with Steve Jobs. Although Apple just became the largest market cap company in the world, the company as "King of the Hill" has become an enormous target for competition to chip away at pieces of the business. Without Steve Jobs as the CEO "King of the Hill," much of the frenzy factor will be gone.

For the outstanding CEO, frenzy is a fact of life, some more frenzied than others. The keen senses that place value on products, services and people also place fear that someone will steal from your plate that which you think you earned and must protect lest you and your people will be left to starve!

Young CEO's like Jobs in his first stint and Bill Gates early in his career evidence frenzy in what is perceived to be brash or even arrogant behavior. Seasoned CEO's tend to accommodate the same frenzy with a calm exterior that belies their experiences in dealing with assorted enemies. I remember feeling somehow understanding when a book describing the management style of Attila the Hun suggested, "It is not enough to win, others must lose." Whether wild or calm on the outside, the frenzy many CEO's feel on the inside is explosive.

Oddly, in my own experience, there was a confidence in our team that often led me to invite competition to our business. Somehow it seemed that if they saw firsthand what we did, how we did it and the talent it took to accomplish it, they would leave feeling less adequate. This was especially true regarding specialty niches within the various companies that always seemed to account for 20% of the business yet 80% of the profit. For me, it was akin to suggesting that this special niche status was ours alone. You could see it, but, you could never be good enough to have "it." Most successful CEO's do not share such a willingness to expose their insides.

On the other hand when someone left our business, with technical knowledge gained and customer relationships sponsored, if they chose to compete directly via their own new venture, there existed a desire to destroy. The same fierceness did not exist if they simply left to join a competitor, recruited or on their own accord. In those cases, it was easy to simply justify the departure as owing to relationships or opportunity, not a threat to our very existence. With direct competition from their own new venture, it was as if the departing associate was saying that we were vulnerable, beatable. For me, the frenzy for preventing success in such competitor circumstances was as strong as the concern for preserving customer and supplier relationships at a level better than any competitor. I am sure that the following perspective will receive criticism for the direct approach to an almost always dangerous and ugly concept, vengeance.

It seems to me that anger cannot serve you. Vengeance, on the other hand seems to serve a purpose if doled out with considerable forethought. Where anger scrambles our patterns of thinking, vengeance can lead to victory. Still, vengeance should never be taken lightly. Consider the plan of action carefully and completely. What may seem like the perfect path for destroying opposition may in fact simply invigorate them. The implications must include consideration for collateral concern by people not presently involved. Unintended consequences might include an increase in support from people sympathetic to your damaged competitor. Customers, suppliers and your own associates must understand the nature and depth of your actions.

My advice is to plan vengeance such that reprisal is not possible. In itself, this may be so difficult that the very prospect eliminates the value of the option of vengeance. Anger, moreover creates an explosion that seems near impossible to direct.

From frenzy to family, it is ultimately important and rewarding to truly view your associates near the importance of your family. This is obviously in sharp contrast to the view espoused above regarding competition. Very early in my career, a long term employee of the factory within which I had just been promoted from factory worker to product estimating trainee taught me a very good lesson. When I made the move from shop to office, I bought new clothes, new shoes and brought along a beamingly bright attitude. The problem was that this very long term female employee (M) seemed to be a detractor from my first encounter. Only after enduring numerous negative comments received indirectly from fellow employees did I work up the nerve to ask her (M) what I had done to earn her distain. It turned out that prior to what I thought was our first encounter, (M) had told me she knew my older sister from their high school years. When she saw my sister some weeks later and asked if I had mentioned her, my sister said NO! Further, it seemed to (M) that each time I passed by her, I completely ignored her. What struck me was that this long term, happily married family woman had seen me a "little brother" type who had shunned her attempts at support by simply paying little attention. I embedded my experience with (M) as an example that taught me that no one should be discounted, for their sake and for mine. When I added what I learned from Dale Carnegie's "How to Win Friends and Influence People" a light went on in my brain that I have tried to keep bright in all communications.

My approach to communication has been very open, some would say to a fault. My belief has been that customers, associates, suppliers and investors benefit from reality, whether good or bad:

1. Customers and suppliers will value you most when you inform them of your plans and especially when you remedy mistakes that have hurt them.
2. Associates will give you real commitment if they are kept apprised of business performance and promise.
3. Investors relate to 1 and 2 in the same manners as all other players.

My observation has been that people who manage mostly by the numbers can perform efficiently but, they lose the important chance to truly connect with their audiences.

The key to familial relations seemed to be initial consideration followed by ongoing respect. As a solo salesman, it seemed to me that my focus had to be simple, get an order. As a manager, leverage in overall performance occurred when I was able to get everyone, or at least most everyone, to focus on the goals we established. It sounds almost ridiculously simple but, such consideration takes considerable discipline. The constant reminder had to be that if I watched out for me, the benefit came from a single effort. If everyone watched out for me, there was an army moving toward the goal. So, while my success was initially based on the ability to sell, alliances built through consideration fostered support rather than suspicion and even contempt.

The above are simple observations and outlines regarding the top role in most businesses. Many of my own views are located at the end of the Influencer chapter where I attempt to share the impact of my experiences and observations.

Marketing

Although marketing is an operating function it also supersedes strategy in hierarchy because it is the basis for establishing presumed or quantified value. Business is rooted in marketing and marketing is not sales. Marketing is not even a distant cousin to sales. Marketing is objective, analytical and then deductive. Marketing, paraphrasing Peter Drucker is quantifying what the customer perceives to be of value. Value whether in product or service is simple requisite. Without value, someone is left to sell a scheme or a widget with no function.

Marketing is not innovation but certainly leads to innovation. Marketing can look at what exists and what existing customers may perceive to be definable enhancements that would increase value. Marketing can ask non-customers what they value in such a manner that products and services can be introduced to them, changed or created for them.

Marketing can also simply ascertain and define what may be of value from a singular perspective; that of the innovator. The key in all cases is value. Whether by data or perception, the ability to delineate what is of or may be of value is marketing.

In the age where information is so broadly available, it is likely that marketing as a separate function will retain little value. The tools used to ask, analyze and make recommendations are no longer specialized. Search engines allow us to ask questions about people and products in near infinite detail.

Marketing for the innovator and entrepreneur also has a raw edge. It is subjective in the view, most often from the outside, that value will exist in an offering. While still marketing, this is the risky business of people, who bet all, only to lose all most of the time and change the world some of the time.

Marketing looks at the world, the nation, the group, the individual and asks again and again, what will the customer value. In asking the questions it is important to ask, who is the customer? The definitions are basic, location and individual profile data create a summary. Marketing exists exclusively to view and analyze what is on the outside of the business.

Within marketing, there is a depth to "why" that goes beyond most consideration, achieving at almost any level, with almost any subject, is enhanced when we persistently ask "why". The incessant habit of asking why does not have to be obvious to those around us. Recall if you will the number of times a young child will ask, "Why?" Most answers are followed by the youngsters asking, "but why?" Often, when explanation is met with exhaustion, we, as adults, finally say, "because!" That may even get expanded to "because I said so!"

Why is a compelling word laced with curiosity, persistence, expansion and implication, a heightened prospect for action? When Einstein said that imagination is more important than knowledge, consider that he was just looking at what existed and what had gone before and constantly asked why. The three letter question is not simple, seldom conclusive, almost always the genesis for a new question, why?

Most cultures precluded fully considering the question, why. Aristocracy, dictatorship and rigid traditions placed boundaries on what was considered fair game. The freedoms that are guaranteed in America allow the question, why, to be a given, even an expectation.

Also within marketing, there are no destinations only locations. The word destination has no basis in fact. Destination denotes something finite. Nothing earthly is fixed. A blade of grass grows. Knowledge grows. Within any group the slightest change in perspective by any one individual changes the group.

Even in Abraham Maslow's fictitious Eupsyschia, the perfect assembly of self-actualized individuals would fail once the actual gathering occurred. Surely, one of the self-actualized people would seek greater status, more control than his/her peers. Destinations perceived to be fixed are only locations where change is constant, even if subtle.

Flexibility is an inherent requirement for survivability. Staying attuned to change requires keen observation, absorption, analysis, implication and action. The slightest miscue can cause fatal derailment.

Oddly, the concept of destination is close to the concept of perfection. Recall that DesCartes suggested that the concept of perfection could be imagined but not located in any earthly sense. Therefore, perfection must only exist in God. It is interesting to consider the implications of attempting to achieve perfection or locating a destination. While DesCartes concluded that the concept of perfection proved the existence of God, no similar conclusion, to my knowledge has been made regarding destination. Thus, it is reasonable to conclude as a mere extension that the concept of destination as a finite location can only exist in that which we call Heaven. Therefore, concept proves existence. All other areas of earthly focus regarding destination are as impossible as perfection was for DesCartes.

In marketing, deductions from data combine history with conjecture to create plans. Plans are created by innovators using research to design and then sell. In my experience a rather unique set of data related to the category and size shoes customers purchased. In addition to the location of the customer, at Eastbay, selling over 200,000 pairs of shoes size 12 to size 20 suggested we were selling to someone who was likely tall. If the zip code pointed to a dominant basketball market and the shoe was a basketball shoe, we were selling to a tall basketball player in a market which produced competitive basketball ball players. So, who was this person? Who did this person know? Where might this person go next?

Further, unlike retailers, we knew who you were, where you lived, what you bought, when you bought and how often you purchased. To our surprise, buyers of wrestling products were the most prolific buyers in multi-sports.

With marketing data we could decide which customers should receive which mailings. As a result, we created a response rate above any direct marketer we knew in the day in any industry. To our amazement, none of the athletic brands sought to benefit from what we knew. One would have thought they would have tried to buy access at a level that allowed them to seed, expose and target with the aim of a rifle. Instead, the shot gun approach to advertising saw imagery in media win out over our approach. We never pushed the value of what we knew beyond suggesting we could sell to their target audience. Because so many of our buyers were minors, we never wanted parents to think we were pushing the children. The value of any customer is multi-faceted and must be considered in its entirety.

Within marketing, knowledge has many facets. It can help us to create. It can help us control. It can help us confuse, destroy or enlighten. When knowledge is gained in most instances, it has no intrinsic value. Unless it is used, knowledge is of course just so much matter. Imagination in all matters is the beginning of consideration for what is possible. Imagination parents innovation. Comparatively, knowledge regarding business relates to what exists and should be considered regarding who it affects and how it affects them and the enterprise.

Too often, knowledge once gained is ignored or improperly considered. Only when we train ourselves to consider the implications of all information do we maximize our chances for continuing success. Even the brightest bulb in the box has no value until we connect it and use it.

Research & Design

R & D exists as Marketing's engineering sibling. Frankly, the function should be renamed Innovation and Design (I&D) with research occurring exclusively within the realm of marketing. With the study of market variables, or simply the perception of what might create, enhance or excite consumers, products and services are created and enhanced in I & D. The more defined the need, the less risky the innovation.

The classic route to innovation is to view what exists with curiosity about how to improve products or services. Better, cheaper, faster, bigger, smaller and new are but a few of the terms that come to mind. Volume, necessity, comfort and luxury are all qualifiers.

Like marketing design requires a focus on the customers perspective of value. Unlike marketing, innovation often goes to perception rather than deduction. Henry Ford suggested that if he had asked the market what was needed, the response would have been a faster horse. But Ford had not created the automobile. Ford improved the processes by which automobiles were produced. True innovation, where something new is created in a void is incredibly rare. To have the imagination to create something truly novel likely requires a mind that is ill fitted for fitting into the existing world. It seems to me that curiosity is a better servant that pure creativity. There is simply too much energy needed to create versus improve. In all cases, the willingness to take risk and produce work energy is tough enough to engender.

When I wrote the white paper "Internet Retail/Groceries In, Garbage Out," which appears later in the Influencers section, I was curious about the changes I saw as imminent with the increasing use of the internet. What I failed to do was risk a substantial amount on the changes that seemed certain. The value of the company was a fear factor as much as an enticer. Although we had started selling online before almost any U.S. retailer, we not only did not mention it in the script of our September, 1995 IPO, we had very few questions about online sales from IPO Roadshow attendees. Like most new frontiers, excitement was balanced by fear of the unknown. While everyone in the athletic products world chattered about the implications of online selling, to my knowledge, only one person decided to dump his old world and adopt what it appeared the market was trending toward. Michael Rubin was the youngest entrepreneur we knew in the early 1990's. Rubin bought and sold distressed inventory creating a credible business while in his teens and early twenties. Then, in 1995, Rubin created Global Sports Inc. to entice retailers to use him to fulfill their online sales. He foresaw the same shift we saw but, Michael Rubin dumped his old shoe sales business and jumped at the building shift toward online selling. With all of the challenges of growth, Rubin built GSI Commerce into a formidable company. After numerous acquisitions and an initial public offering, GSI Commerce was sold to EBAY for $2.4 billion. The market had all of the data to suggest that the new internet frontier would produce gold, but, few existing players had what it took to change their game plans enough to win in the new world of commerce. Generally, it seems people are focused on the now. With keen observation, marketing criteria causes a few people to consider now and project next with work applied to their vision. In a more autonomous business world, the questions regarding value will belong to each of us.

Sales

While marketing seeks information from the outside, analyzes, dissects and derives conclusions, sales acts on those determinations with actions targeting customers and non-customers.

With market data regarding customers, competition and economics, sales, along with general management and finance management sets pricing for products and services.

Advertising attempts to define value and differentiate offerings with the hope that customers and more importantly, non-customers will be impacted in a meaningful and memorable way.

But, more on pricing, advertising and other sales functions later. There is an age old saying related most often to fundraising and selling: "with all things equal, people will choose to work with people they like." And so, in a practical sense, it pays to approach selling with an effort to be liked.

For me, the best sales tool I was ever given was Dale Carnegie's book, "How to Win Friends and Influence People." When taken to the extreme, Carnegie students can seem phony and contrived in nature. But, when we simply consider the perspective of those with whom we have contact, reciprocal consideration is a natural result.

Going beyond the Golden Rule, intimate, immediate consideration should be given to the possible results your words and actions may bring. The calculation for possible effects is considered a form of manipulation by some people. To this I say, so what! If my goal is to motivate a preferred response, consideration of factors like gratification, reward and frequency are all quite reasonable. A checkpoint for me in most interpersonal exchanges occurs when I do a mental check by asking myself if I am talking at you, into you or indeed, with you. A drill sergeant talks at you. A good teacher talks into you, looking for ways to connect. A good partner in any endeavor talks with you, actively listens, responds with an effort to promote positive continuing results. To create a lasting effect in sales relationships, it important to preconceive how and why the possible partnerships may have merit.

While it almost goes without saying, I will say it anyway; partnerships benefit from personal consideration. Personal consideration may not be reciprocal but again, so what! If you remember important dates, important events and important people in your life, the result will be positive. In the past, I would spend hours each January transcribing important dates on my paper calendar. Today, technology makes the process easy. The ease may in fact lessen the value over time but, it is still important to maintain intense consideration. Soon, everyone will automatically know and be reminded of everyone else's birthday, anniversary, hire date, etc.

A lifelong lesson occurred when I was 24 and trying to make my mark as a salesman. The 1973 Arab Oil Embargo created a need to produce more energy efficient buildings. We produced aluminum windows and exterior wall systems for the architectural construction market. By structure aluminum conducted rather than blocked energy transmission. To create a thermal barrier, two pieces of aluminum were attached with a vinyl connector piece continuously crimped or rolled together in order to break transmission of exterior heat or cold.

The product that I was trying to promote to architects used a poured in place polyurethane that, once cured, held the inside and outside aluminum together. Because polyurethane cured like concrete into a perceived to be brittle material, architects were leery that it would crack and the window or window wall would fall apart and crash to the ground below.

As an enthusiastic salesman, I targeted one of the largest hospital architectural firms in America as the prime target for our products, Henningson, Durham and Richardson (HDR), Omaha, Nebraska. Each month I would drive 12 hours from Wausau, Wisconsin to Omaha to visit HDR and other architectural firms located in Omaha. The problem for me was that HDR only approved one system for the very pricey windows that went into the hospitals they designed, the vinyl connector system. So, each month I would ask to see the Chief Specification writer and each month I was politely turned away. Finally, Carl Agerbeck, a crusty crew cut Chief Specification writer agreed to give me fifteen minutes to pitch the merits of our revolutionary, but suspect thermal barrier systems.

When I entered his large office, the phone rang within seconds. Mr. Agerbeck listened, asked questions and began to visibly boil. After five of my fifteen minutes elapsed, he hung up. He said his wife had called regarding a terrible car service experience at the local Chrysler dealer. I listened quietly as he vented about the declining nature of quality and service from Chrysler, the only brand he owned in 1974 and the Agerbeck family owned two Chryslers. When he finally calmed enough to look at the clock he said that he was sorry but the time was up and he needed to go to another meeting. I had wanted to interrupt, to somehow convey that I had spent many months driving 600 miles each way to have this meeting, but, I felt I should not speak. I expressed my hope that American companies would see the need for quality with Japan gaining credibility. I left a flyer on our product and asked if I could call on him another time, any time? He said he would call me and two weeks later, he did call. At the next meeting, he assembled 10 architects and spec writers to hear my product story and grill me with questions. Subsequently, we became the second company approved to bid HDR projects. The following year we provided windows for 43 hospitals making HDR our number one architectural ally. Carl Agerbeck sponsored my membership in the Construction Specifications Institute and I became an Omaha Chapter member. I was able to discuss the merits of all window and wall systems with every firm in Omaha which was a hotbed for architects, including powerhouses like Leo A. Daly, Inc.

Carl and I remained in close contact until his retirement. After he retired, my company purchased his privately owned antique office furniture in remembrance. For me, the remembrance will always be that the customer sets the agenda and the priorities. Listening is an active skill that requires us to put our heads inside our customers' heads. When accomplished with sincerity, all things being equal, people will buy from people they like. As a postscript, because the vinyl thermal barrier window was losing a monopoly when Carl approved us, they went to all ends to try to stop us. When they went over Carl's head to protest, they were soon excluded from bidding, no longer liked!

In sales, relationships are more important than products. I know that sounds a bit strange but it has been true. There were many times when we designed or produced a poor performing products within the companies for which I had responsibility. I had learned from my first boss that rather than fret over the expenses caused by remedial work, we should look at repairs as our chances to shine. We certainly did not want to make poor products, but, with products designed, engineered and produced to custom sizes for almost every job, the numbers of chances to make mistakes was exponentially higher than for companies who produced standard products.

When we learned that a product leaked, peeled, whistled, or simply did not operate smoothly, we cheerfully sent a crew to make the fix. While competitors were contentious and combative, we assumed the problems were ours to fix and consequently contractors, architects and owners loved us. We were almost never the least expensive product. We were good producers but, not great producers. We were, more than any construction products manufacturer we knew, the most dependable product producer. With New York City as our biggest market, by nature, an intensely suspect customer found us to be a very refreshing supplier. As a sales tool, customer service should not simply be espoused and sold; it should be shown in all you provide the customer. The sense that your lasting relationship is so important that you will assume the obligation for satisfying needs will cause a reciprocal desire to see you survive and prosper.

In a simple example of salesmanship, I was given the Chicago area as my first sales territory when I was promoted from the factory to construction products estimator. I was told that my customer, Builders Architectural Products (BAP) was owned by a tough negotiator named Gerry Goldman. Further, his top salesman, Vern Jensen needed more prices on more projects than reasonable. In addition, both men were near the end of their careers while I was just beginning. I did my best to accommodate the needs of my customer no matter how tough some days seemed. About a year after being assigned to B.A.P., Gerry Goldman pressed me hard for a lower price on a project he claimed he needed for the very survival of B.A.P. Calculating that the required price would be below our costs, I decided to acquiesce and give Gerry that price he said he needed. Then, in order to satisfy our company Presidents intense concern for my decision, I volunteered my time to do as many of the shop functions I had learned over six years as a factory worker to reduce our cost to produce the job. Some months later when

B.A.P. secured the contract on a much bigger and better project, Goldman sent the order to our company President with special note, "10% has been added to your quote in recognition of exceptional past service. " While this action did not result in any immediate gain for me, it was etched into my experience. When, at age 26, I was chosen to run a division of our public company, this simple act was referred to as above and beyond. For me, it was little time spent for much gained in my career.

As personal as sales relationships can be, pricing concerns for products are generally more strategic than personal. Unless your niche is highly specialized and/or technical, pricing strategy should strive to own the world, not just your neighborhood.

To defeat or even prevent competition, as soon as you know your innovative entrepreneurial enterprise is returning profit above average you should:

1. Closely calculate the potential cost of growth.
2. Begin to cut prices in order to fight potential competitors from seeing too much allure.

The possible qualifiers to this suggestion are solid mechanical patents or near insurmountable barriers to entry. Pharmaceutical companies often enjoy the former while jumbo jet manufacturers might be an example of the latter. In most ventures there is no such advantage. In my career, two of the businesses had distinct competitive advantages. Experience in the earlier venture had an effect on how we faced competition in the production of wooden venetian blinds. Interior designer firms in the Pacific Design Center in Hollywood/Beverly Hills along with similar customers in New York's D&D building made our challenge singular, make more blinds. At the time, 1978, prices for most window coverings products averaged a few dollars per square foot. We had no idea where to price wood blinds but needed to, somehow control volume. So, I continually raised our price until we reached $12 per square foot, an amount that at the time seemed absurd.

But, demand continued to build. Within a year, our little wooden build manufacturing company was providing the highest return on investment of any division of public company, Apogee Enterprises.

We became the talk of the design industry. The company name, Nanik, pronounced nan-ick became so stylish for designers that I was corrected numerous times by designers who insisted the company name was pronounced Nan-eek, a bit more French, a bit more sophisticated. I just smiled and the register kept going cha-ching!

With all of our success, I was promoted to group President in 1982, at age 31. I hurriedly guided our group from 3 solid divisions to as many as 12 companies. Start-ups and acquisitions seemed to occur every few months. What I lost sight of and simply missed was the effect success was having on Nanik.

What distributors, designers and customers saw as attractive about wood blinds, competitors were seeing too! Competitors saw the public reporting of incredible profit as too enticing to ignore. When Hunter Douglas, the largest window covering manufacturer of the time, offered to buy Nanik, we declined. While they already produced wood blinds, they wanted our Nanik name and the aura it provided. After declining there offer, we saw a dramatic decrease in Hunter Douglas pricing and a dramatic increase in the variety and quantity of products they produced. As other manufacturers in the industry came to see that this specialty product could be copied, we saw the business quickly become a commodity. Today, Apple holds a position similar but thousands of time more significant than Nanik. When you enjoy the margins Apple enjoys, competitors can afford to spend huge sums in order to try to get a bite out of the Apple. While pricing is discussed as a sales consideration, I by no means suggest that setting price is an exclusive task within the sales function. Rather, sales are the touch points where customer's perspectives and competitor actions are most visible. As a conduit of information, the salesperson serves as a catalyst. Marketing data, accounting data and sales perspective are ultimately considered by general management where pricing decisions ultimately must be made.

As noted earlier, advertising seeks to define value and differentiate offerings in meaningful and/or memorable ways. As a sensory function, advertising is art. As a means of sharing information, advertising is data differentiation, sometimes by competitive comparison.

The migration to autonomy in functions has very little bearing on advertising; it is already an outside resource for most companies. What will likely change is the advertising agency as we know it today? Graphics, writing and all other ad agency functions should be easily segmented and rejoined wherever talents are needed. Like an orchestral group, delineation of roles and sequence and harmony should be simple.

As an executive I developed my own set of opinions and biases regarding advertising. Since so much of advertising is art there really can be few rules about what works and what does not work, only opinions and results.

The basic questions of who, what, when, where and why are always a good place to start. In the construction world served early in my career, the message I heard from architects, contractors and owners was that they disliked door, window and roof suppliers because their products leaked. The messages therefore needed to focus on quality and even more important, reliability. In the interior design business, the "it" factor was key to being fashionable. We won advertising awards with our agency for ads that showed wood venetian blinds hanging from trees with the caption, "A warm natural way to dress windows has come out of the woods." In our athletic products business, Eastbay, where the target was the 14-24 year old athlete, covers that inspired and entertained were given nearly as much work as the products that went inside the catalog. Comic book like characters and real star athletes were points of connection.

Consideration for what is compelling seems to me to be more important than just getting noticed even though the old adage "first you have to get their attention" is true. It is rare for something like the AFLAC duck or the Geico gecko to become iconic. It seems more practical to compel with phrases like "Just Do It," "Finger lickin good," or "You're in good hands," just to name a few. The taboos for me are based on my own gut feel. Never make an ad about food with the live animal that must be killed for your enjoyment. To see a juicy hamburger with cattle in the scene simply does not work for me. Never make fun of a real name; someone has that name and a family, friends and associates. Don't try to impress your audience with words they are not likely to understand. When a friend, Lou Gentine's enormous cheese business used the word "Persnickety" as the key ad word, I was vocally concerned. With mouthwatering imagery of cheese, persnickety did not cut it for me.

We may soon see that the only acceptable producer based ads are informational ads that tell us what is coming. What is coming is news. What is here is no longer news and we will only accept hearing about it if we want to hear about it. It would seem that matrices that create only specific access to the exact information we seek is what would be of greatest value. Again, Peter Drucker defined marketing within the concern for determining what is of value to the customer. There may even be value in further distinction of marketing from all sales related functions. If we eliminate all sales tools, especially advertising, from the marketing function, marketing work can become clearer. Market, that segment we choose to serve, is expansive enough not to be contaminated by other tasks. Marketing should be data concentric! As information continues toward ubiquity, consumers may find all advertising to be trite and self-serving. The balance between a willingness to be hooked and disdain for being interrupted should be an interesting migration.

Traditionally, retention programs have been part of the sales function. In the migration toward autonomy, it is likely that affinity and retention efforts will be performed in applications provided in various boilerplate forms in various industries.

Except in the most technical businesses, for sales to migrate to autonomy should be quite simple. The model for an independent function has existed in the distribution world where independent representatives offer a variety of products from companies. With information options, the onus will be on the supplier to provide incentive, distinction and consistent performance in products and services. The onus will still be on the salesperson to connect with his/her customer. Strategies must be linked to actions which get inside the customers wallet, head and heart to create a positive experience which the customers want to replicate again and again and again.

When you consider that with all things being equal, people give to and buy from people they like, it is incumbent on each of us to constantly consider how we are and may be received. I have always suggested that we must carefully package, review and sell ourselves and our stories. Even more important is the absolute requirement to never buy your own story. Only a fool buys his/her own story!

Operating Tips

It is easier to describe what good management is not than what good management is. It is not a science. It is not a profession. It really is not even a practice. Management requirements are too circumstantial, too human to be fit into anything more than broad concepts. That is not to say that broad concepts are unimportant in framing at least partially what management is.

Management employs capital and human assets. Decisions regarding plant, property and equipment (P, P & E) involve critical criteria for the manager. Creating and/or choosing the type, quality and expenses related is both science and practical gamble.

While plant, property and equipment are most commonly referred to in accounting vernacular as PP&E, each has a very real management implication in every business. No matter how simple, every business is located somewhere, on some land, using some devices to complete the intended tasks necessary to produce a product or service. Management decisions that employ too much, too little or inappropriate PP& E are a threat to survival. Management must ascertain the appropriate PP&E risk at any point in time needed to succeed.

In a general management career that spanned nearly a quarter century, there were many PP&E decisions that loomed large when faced. Systems, pre-press, machinery and buildings decisions were ever present. In most cases, we considered appropriateness for capital expenditures on a must have, can justify or nice to have basis. By requiring three categories, we could separate criteria in a meaningful way. "Must have" column items were just that, replacing critical capital items with viable replacements needed to stay in business. Return ratios were almost meaningless, unless exiting a product offering was a consideration.

"Can justify" capital request items were things that fit a column that could be justified by a payback analysis that stood the test of scrutiny. A new version of some machine that produced a product better or faster usually fit this column. Competitor intelligence often brought awareness of new machines or newer systems that would fit the "can justify" column.

"Nice to have" items were only considered in very profitable periods when cash was abundantly available. If the return on investment from productivity gains was in excess of the return cash garnered sitting in the bank, "nice to have" capital expenditures won approval as investments in the future.

The most memorable capital expenditure consideration in my career relate to the creation of equipment for automating the production of finishing wood slats for venetian blinds. Remember that wood venetian blinds had not been produced in the United States since the pre-Civil War period. At age 26, with a very small staff, we attempted to satisfy interior designer demands for product by hand staining 1" wide by 1/8" thick basswood slats. On makeshift racks we dried, lacquered, flipped and lacquered both sides followed by hand waxing with steel wool and rag rubs.

We were so busy selling and producing wood blinds that I was not aware of much that was occurring in the world outside our tiny corner of a window manufacturing plant. On a usual day where designers called to complain about how long their orders for custom wood blinds were taking, I received what would later become a memorable call. The designer said he was remodeling the Borden House in New York City for a very special client. He said his client was planning a Halloween party and would like to come to the phone to ask me for help in getting the custom blinds shipped in time to make his party. He said his clients name was Bobby DeNiro. When Mr. DeNiro came to the phone, he simply said something like, "Hello Mr. Colcord, I would very much appreciate anything you can do to speed up this order." I responded that we would surely do our best similar to all responses that I made to such requests.

When I hung up, I asked my assistant if she knew of a guy in New York named DeNiro. This was 1978 and she said something to the effect that I must be living under a rock. She said DeNiro and Barbara Streisand were the only actors making $1 million per movie.

I digress but, it is simply meant to show how all-consuming business can be when you are fighting to survive. Because we did work hard, our parent company, Apogee Enterprises approved the capital expenditures we requested for a new plant and new equipment. The problem for us was there was no equipment to buy.

In fact, in 1978, basswood slats were only produced for making bee hives. Not only did we not have equipment to cut, punch, stain and lacquer wood slats, during bee hive production season, there was no capacity for making the slats for our designer wood venetian blinds. So, learning first about how wood behaved and then enticing people to make it into various lengths of un-warped 1 inch and later 2 inch slats was the first challenge. There was no management convention to consider beyond a growing need for supply that was not met by availability. The key is often simply to be responsive. The various considerations regarding building an organization, fortifying industry position, and continuous innovation and improvement are futile. In initial operating priorities you must first respond and then survive.

As an operator, once you survival appears likely, bolstering your prospects for continuing success is in order. In the CEO section, many of the suggestions for developing strategy and setting objectives are discussed. In this operating section, another area of concern relates to all of the meeting related to almost every aspect of the business.

Meetings

Within a more autonomous environment, it is likely that the pressure to meet less and produce more will be a self-fulfilling prophecy. To make meetings more productive, there are a few recommendations that should still hold true. This may be too obvious but, I will continue anyway.

In my years as a group president at Apogee, I was usually frustrated by the number and length of meetings. While I never wanted to offend the person who initiated the call to meet, I often found myself wondering what I was doing in this meeting. What could anyone possibly gain from this undirected, unending gathering of talent? I wanted to scream, but, screaming was not on the agenda. In fact, typically there was no agenda. Eventually, without reference to any offenders, I simply listed the obvious concerns that I had related to meetings.

Too often, meetings:

1. Had no clearly stated purpose
2. Had no written, shared agenda
3. Did not start on-time
4. Had individuals arrive late
5. Suffered through pontificating at the podium
6. Wandered off the mark with no sideboard for handling the wanderers unrelated agendas

7. No control of contributors
8. No notes on what was happening
9. No summary of actionable items
10. No follow up items
11. No adhered to end time
12. No shared minutes

With all the listed concerns, I did not want to summarily cast aspersions on many of my people. They were after all, my people. So, I looked for an academic meetings course which I could use to rein in the meetings culprits. While I have retained no notes on the few day courses I found somewhere, I do recall that I was basically able to deal with each of the above concerns by pointing to the academic expertise learned in my Meetings Meetings. So trite, but so needed were the following:

1. A call to meet needs to be defined by a clear subject.
2. Whether before or at the meeting, a clear agenda must be shared with all attending.
3. Meetings begin at the appointed time.
4. Late attendees may be welcomed but, they are not allowed to be disruptive.
5. If you are running a meeting, follow the agenda, seek input, suggest conclusions and remember that you are not running for political office.
6. When participants inevitably wander off the agenda with their own agendas, a sideboard is used to quickly write down the unrelated item. Politely or firmly let the participant know that if time allows, you will address the written concern at the end of the agenda or after the meeting.
7. To keep control it is often appropriate to interject a summary of what has been said with notice that you must move forward to new agenda items or new contributions, a nice way of saying "shut the hell up!"
8. A large monitor or tablet tells participants what is being summarized contemporaneously.

9. Where possible, following itemized summary items, actionable items are noted.
10. Agreed upon timelines and follow up dates are noted.
11. When the end time arrives, end the meeting. Some may agree to stay on for continuation or conclusion but, all must be excused without any sense of guilt.
12. Whether or not meeting objectives are met, all participants should receive minutes with summary comments and next steps.

For many, these meeting suggestions are so elementary that they could go without mention. For others, they may be a route to better, more productive gatherings.

Whether focused on meeting standards or other issues never, ever, forget perspective. Carnegie may have taken winning friends to extremes but, the concept is as important as any you can ever learn. Do unto others does not even begin to go far enough. You live at a different level than the person you affect. Social, economic, business, personal circumstances are all different than yours.

While each function in business may differ from one company to the next, below are brief comments related to two functions that may change dramatically and quickly.

Engineering

While Engineers might object, my contention is that Engineering is also a subset of Marketing. Engineering is entrusted with critical considerations like functionality and competitive advantage. This does not diminish the significant role engineering plays in the business. Design engineering, structural engineering, mechanical engineering, industrial engineering, etc., etc., etc., all have critical tasks in how things can and do work. My point is that whatever works, works for all customers. Whatever works has value for a customer. Anything that has value for a customer is a marketing consideration. Unlike Research and Design, Engineering should not be expensed as a Marketing cost. In this case, Engineering is simply suggested as linked to Marketing as a subset. The costs and actual reporting for engineering are still inside costs, operating costs. The operating tip in an autonomous age is that Engineering is one of the most critical tasks we should consider. So, considering where we connect Engineering is critical.

Information Technology

Another operating tip is to begin to decrease the importance of Information Technology as a distinct function. Certainly, information will still need to organized, processed and stored in an effective manner. However, in an age where more is done by autonomous contributions, there should be less need for centralized information. While we will not slough off past results, we will be more likely to search for new tools and new contributors for every task at hand. The rapid change in experience and improvement in tools will make much of our history obsolete far more quickly than in the past.

Human Resource Management

I have been concerned for many years about the evolution of the human resource function within organizations. What existed for years as a co-ordination function has been elevated into a key management function which sadly is far more akin to consulting than to an executive task within an enterprise.

When Human Resources departments dealt with the benefits research, suggestions and co-ordination, the administrative function seemed to be a great assist to executives. Somewhere between its administrative function and today's management role, HR immersed itself in the task of surveying and surmising what was important for recruiting, selecting, training and motivating people.

For me, an important contribution I hope to make for the improvement in business performance would be the destruction of Human Resources as we have come to know it today. Protocol, legalese, contempt and arrogance have all too often replaced compassion in addressing the human resource function. To be sure, there are outstanding individuals in human resource management today. My contention is that they are good people, poorly placed.

When top management accepted the HR function as it is most often seen today, they likely did so in order to avoid many of the uncomfortable tasks related to search, interviewing, selection, training, motivating, retaining and sometimes outplacing people.

The problem seems to me to be that once you have created something of value for a customer, be it product or service, all of the human resource selection and development issues are critical for the very reason the business exists, to create and retain customers.

While the chief executive need not perform human resource tasks for every employee of the enterprise, the manager responsible for the performance within each specific function should be responsible. Assignment of these critical tasks is not delegation, in my humble opinion, it is abdication. So much is lost to management that work becomes inherently more difficult, not less difficult as a result.

What do I mean by the last statement? First, recruitment and screening show the executive what is not available. Who are all the non-hires and why are they inappropriate for your organization? Knowing that non-hires exist enhances the likelihood that you will treat hires as appropriate for your team, good bets to build upon. Just as every line on an income statement should be owned by someone in the business, every hire should be connected to someone who can affect the training, development and motivation from the start of the work relationship. It is incorrect to say "this is business, not personal" when considering human resource management. It is personal in a vital manner.

When you envision what might be ideal in a candidate and personally see what is available, what is <u>not</u> available may be the best impetus for you to create training tools to enhance skills in the hire who was not the ideal performer you did not find.

A major factor in leadership is the sense that you are connected. To start a relationship where you are handed to the executive by human resources simply eliminates a huge connection opportunity. The fact that, he/she looked for, interviewed and chose me is a bond. That is far more complex than selecting the candidate from the three or so offered by HR. It is my contention that remembering something about someone may be the trigger which creates enthusiasm for performance beyond anyone's wildest dreams, including their own.

The origin of today's Human Resource Management (HRM) likely first gained prominence at the Harvard Business School in 1981. For me, 1981 was three years after I had begun running a business when, at 26, I was given the chance to run a start-up business within a public company, Apogee Enterprises (APOG) called Nanik. Again, Nanik was the first manufacturer to produce wooden venetian blinds in America since the Civil War. With no processes, equipment or experienced staff, it was a bit like the Wild Wild West. I distinctly recall that our young burly shop foreman understood human resource management as picking up a rowdy, young worker, holding him above his head and telling him that if he would not agree to start listening, he would drop him on the floor! As the head of the company, I quickly came to realize that human resource management would require training.

When I was first promoted to run a company, I had no understanding of structure regarding selection and training, I only understood that there was work to be done. I distinctly recall that my confusion could only be confronted with two skills, one, the ability to work and two, the ability to sell. Therefore, I alternated between selling our customers on our projected ability to produce with time on the shop floor, making samples for these customers. The other important facet was to sell every employee, every day, on the opportunity we could create if we worked. If Harvard academics were starting their discussions regarding enhancing the status of human resource management, we were not aware of it in the trenches, where work occurred.

While human resource management discussions were also occurring at Michigan and New York schools about the same time, internet search points to the Harvard MBA course with greatest detail. Inherently, an educational institution does not seem to be the place where practical management operating functions will be enhanced. Rather, the field of play seems to be a better place for standards and practices to be conceived, tried and proven effective, or ineffective. Because I had worked part-time and then full time in a factory for six years, I saw the "field of play" from more angles than many managers of my day. I never forgot how smart many of my fellow plant workers were compared to me. They simply chose not to take a path in the work that would cause them to worry more and sleep less with advancement.

As Peter Drucker considered the evolving role of the worker, progress toward the "knowledge worker," as coined by Drucker, meant management needed a new and higher priority regarding human resources.

Drucker said, in Management Challenges for the 21st Century:

> "Managements duty is to preserve the assets of the institution in its care. What does this mean when the knowledge of the individual knowledge worker becomes an asset and, in more and more cases, the main asset of an institution? "

It means management's top priority is to recruit, select, train, monitor and motivate the talent of the organization. In addition, outplacement is a painful but necessary function which should not be delegated. Within the human resource requirement, occasionally, hopefully rarely, someone must be fired. When you fire someone, you are not just affecting a person; you are impacting the individual, the family, the friends, the fellow associates and the future of all of the above! It is very somber, very serious.

Oddly, in my own experience, professional human resource staff members have on numerous occasions found the firing process to be okay and even, sadly, exhilarating. Protocol has the H.R. pro suggesting that he/she needs to sit in on the dismissal in order to properly document the company position. Beyond observation, H.R. should have nothing to do with outplacement. The failure belongs to the manager and to the employee. Neither should be denied the full impact of such a failure. The concern for proper legal handling of outplacement is overshadowed by the need for personal reconciliation by the real stakeholders, the employer and the employee!

When a manager determines that an outplacement is required, it is a terribly serious event for the person who is leaving. When a manager reviews individual performance, the simplest question is, if not here today, would I hire this person for this job. If the role or relationships are deemed to be wrong then change is appropriate. The way that the manager, not an HR person, handles the outplacement is critical.

Getting outplaced, or fired, is worse than enduring a divorce. In a divorce both individuals can reason that they did not fail alone. The anger may be more intense. The lingering sense of loss may be pervasive. But, no matter the feelings, they are not solo, they are shared or at that very least, blamed.

When a person is outplaced, they have been chosen as a failure. It is a singular recognition. No matter how you deliver the news, it will have a lasting impact. The HR consulting world points to the need to assure individuals they are okay, only the role or the relationship or both may be wrong. My perspective, except in very rare egregious cases, was always to look for ways to assure the person being outplaced that they could find a fit. While attitude, skill set and outlook did not fit the role they currently served, surely there was a good fit in another company where he/she should seek employment. Further, in most instances, I would spend whatever time I needed to spend in order to help them connect with a new employer. The gain from such assistance was that other people in my employ felt they would be helped if things went bad for them. Also, our costs for unemployment compensation and prospective legal battles decreased. All I had to do was look for a fit for them and spend a little time promoting them to a new employer.

When we decide to hire someone, we do so with a belief that this person will succeed. Certainly each will need help with training, monitoring and motivation. To suggest that some percent of people must be labeled failures seems very wrong. When I read Jack Welsh's suggestion that employees exist in a 20/70/10 world, I was surprised and almost disgusted. Imagine that you live in a world where each year, 10% of the people must be deemed failures and outplaced. Whether or not the number is correct is meaningless. My guess is that 80% of the people in that company are adversely affected. If only 20% are to be deemed top performers, then, by implication, everyone who is not part of that 20% is at risk. I never wanted anyone we paid to feel anything other than they were on our team. Our job as managers includes monitoring and assessing performance. My contention as noted is that we will find people fitted in the wrong role or wrong relationship. If that occurs, it is incumbent on us to share in recognizing and resolving this failure. Any program that dilutes the significance of such failure is a discredit to the human resource management role.

While pontificating on the logic of reestablishing most human resource functions as inherently each manager's responsibility, a long time business friend objected, giving what he thought was a perfect case for maintaining human resource management as a strategic management function, not simply an administrative task as I was suggesting. He suggested an example of how Human Resource Management should work was evidenced in the business of one of our very good friends. We have known this friend for nearly 25 years. He operates half dozen mini steel mills and is immensely talented and successful. In his circumstance, it was suggested that a few years ago, he invested in the most talented Human Resource manager available, a top notch professional that came with a keen interest in the business, its customers and its associates. She was, in the telling, a wonderful addition to the business. As my friend recounted her performance experience, it was clear to me that this was a rare talent. He went on to suggest that our mutual friend was thrilled by her success in selecting talent ideal for the tasks of the business. She knew what was needed and she developed the resources required to perform at a very high level. She became, according to the business owner, his right hand. I imagined she was a true asset to our friend, further enhanced in value because of his very nature. The owner you see is more introverted and more inclined to technical matters than people matters. So, he had found a human resource manager to supplement what he lacked. He had found, as it has been suggested he said, his right hand. My next question may seem too obvious but, I asked anyway. What happens if he loses his right hand? You see, it is not really attached. It is a supplement. Now, that may be a necessary risk with some functions in the business but, in my view, not with the most important work within the management function. We certainly do hire people for functions not widely performed except by specialists. The accountant, the engineer and the systems professional are all likely to have valuable skills which top management does not have within their own skill set. The difference however is distinct. Tasks are more easily defined and have fewer connections than the function of human resource management. Tasks are things, limited things; human resource management involves risk and reward that encompasses the entire business. When you think of recruitment, selection, placement, training, monitoring and motivating functions, the connection points are far more numerous and complicated than those attached to the tasks. Please understand, as mentioned earlier, this is not to say that the top manager must perform the human resources function for all hires, rather, only for hires reporting directly to him/her and so on throughout the management structure of the organization.

In the 1985 edition preface to Peter Drucker's 1973 book, Management Tasks, Responsibilities and Practices, Dr. Drucker suggests: "Unlike the work of the physician, the stonemason or the lawyer, management must always be done in an organization- that is, with a web of human relations." It is therefore my contention that the touch points, the connections, the importance of the human resource function are too vast, too significant to the organization to be delegated to a separate function.

When you watch a movie, you try to understand the characters. Who are they, where are they from, what has affected them, what do they want and what might they do to get it? In business relationships, as in all relationships, those understandings will help to foster a positive result. Stepping outside your role in every interaction to ascertain the roles of each person involved will increase your ability to create an effective result.

From experience, effective communication is of paramount importance in managing human resources. There are so many things that can go wrong in relationships that businesses are wise to adopt some procedures that can be regularly used, especially in discussing problems. In managing a group of manufacturing companies, it was clear to me that we had grown faster than our supervisory skills had grown. A sense of general discontent on the shop floor was obvious by the way associates would greet each other and me. Because it was common knowledge that I had spent six rather happy years as a part-time and then full-time shop worker, the onus for me was compelling. It seemed that, like many businesses, we promoted good performers to supervisory positions. What we failed to do was train them as supervisors in the same effective manner they had been trained to be producers when they joined what had been a much smaller company. When we set out to find reliable programs to use as a tool for training, we came across a firm in Pittsburgh teachings something called Interaction Management from DDI. When I checked on their status, I saw that DDI shows a tremendous client list. From what I saw however, Apogee and/or Wausau Metals were no longer mentioned. Nonetheless, while I have no materials from the Interaction Management training I took 30 years ago, the basic tenets were simple and have stayed with me. I recall a few weeks of formal training in Pittsburgh, certification as an instructor and my return to Wausau, WI to teach what I had learned to our seventy first line supervisors. First, I gave an extensive session to the company presidents and top management of the companies within the group of firms I served as group President. This was a logical step needed to enlist support such that we all communicated from the same script. The basic criteria seem almost too simple to list, but I will anyway:

1. Be sure to start with a level head, anger will not serve you.
2. State the reason for the discussion.
3. Discuss possible action steps.
4. Agree on a plan, resources needed and acceptable levels of performance that are measurable.
5. Set up time specific follow up date.

My rationale for including this basic interaction information is simple. We assumed good performers would make good supervisors. In fact, good performers who judge others by their own superior performance can be intolerant supervisors unable to empathize with "normal" performance. Good training builds good supervisors. There are certainly a myriad of training tools available to choose from, the point, even in today's knowledge based world is that you should start by choosing something as an aid. Communication in business is a tool and the tool does not come natural to all who must use it. To motivate people, it is important to learn to catch them doing something right.

The vast array of considerations regarding human resource management likely makes this area of concern the most complex within the organization. If you refer back to the Objectives discussion in the CEO chapter, the objective related to Hiring/Interviewing Tips attempts to discuss behavior and skill concerns. Whether conducted by the CEO or shop foreman, the evaluation of talent will have similar criteria. Each hiring manager is looking to add champions. True champions see the goal clearly. True champions attack work with consistency and enthusiasm. True champions are optimistic idiots, monomaniacs and evangelists. True champions say, "Yes we can do this!" True champions not only do not buy their own story, they have a strong sense of self but are dominated by humility and humor. True champions are approachable, nurturing individuals who co-workers look to for help in their efforts to do a good job.

Human resource management is an intense task. Jokingly, or half-jokingly, I suggested many times that as I trained to learn to manage on the job, I may have learned more about psychology than business. While my observations are likely elementary and even trite to a trained psychologist, they may be of practical use for business people.

The notable difference in the way people react to input seems to be a basic way information is processed. While there are varied approaches in most people, there appears to be a propensity in each person to process dominantly either from the inside or the outside. By that, I mean that some people instinctively, almost automatically process input as it relates to them on the inside. Whether positive or negative, the joy or despair appears to be part of their fabric. Those who process input on the outside appear to factor information. How does this affect me, others, how should I react, how will I react? In personality inventories, this has likely been part and parcel to the label, thinker versus feeler. In business, it is a critical consideration for gauging management skills.

There are no absolutes regarding how inside thinkers might succeed as manager, only generalizations. It seemed to me that people who processed information as it relates to them first were more likely to be good performers than good managers. Like the star athlete they needed to push hard to prove their worth. Outside thinkers, processors, seemed to calculate longer, whether contriving or conniving. Again generally, outside thinkers are more likely to recognize that there is leverage when they factor consideration for everyone affected by the matter at hand. Inside thinkers are more likely to simply spring to action.

When I reflect on the failures endured by key contributors I remember always wanting to be supportive if their efforts had appeared reasonable. The standard clichés regarding the value of failures were always quick to be shared. It seems an area where better preparation might help.

Time and again, especially in sports but also in business and personal matters, the impending collapse is the subject of legends. As imminent as collapses are, it seems a proactive approach might help avert a few.

As painful as it is to watch, the aftermath can even be more painful. It does not take a nationally televised interview to understand the pain. Therein, the prospective pain may be an aversion tool. If, in the first moment fear of failure is felt, we do our own post-collapse interview, maybe; just maybe, we can lower the stressors that will otherwise effect performance.

Positive imaging has been used for many years as an aid in performance. See yourself successfully advancing toward your goals with success in every swing, every step every sentence. By so doing, the actual actions will not feel new or foreign.

Preparing to fail should, in rehearsal, image how we will survive. How the short term may hurt but, the long term is still there, still okay. If we do not win, we can usually play again. If we fail to sell, there are other prospective customers and so on. The more quickly and thoroughly we examine the likely real results of failure, the less likely we are to fail. We are likely to breath more freely, move more freely and think and speak with less stress over impending failure.

As the organization evolved in the 20th century, so too did technology. When Drucker used the words knowledge worker, clearly he saw the shift from command/control to a new requirement, more like the conductor of an orchestra, as his example. In the 21st century, how much will management matter? How much must management change? It seems that much of Drucker's orchestra example will be relevant for the manager. It may also come to pass that some of Maslow's description of the "Hierarchy of Needs" may begin again at the bottom for the players in the orchestra. What do I mean by the last statement? Well, when knowledge workers combine to accomplish a task, their roles are no longer perceived as lasting. The sense that you are part of a family will likely decrease more and more over time. The sense that the company will care for you if you do your job is now simply gone. Therefore, the "Physiological" need at the base of Maslow's pyramid will be relevant for the knowledge worker who simply first must be chosen to be part of the team. And no matter how much comfort and satisfaction the worker feels in accomplishing the relevant task, he/she must begin again at the bottom each time new work is begun. This does not mean talented workers, like talented artists in an orchestra, will not be highly sought after, no, rather it means there is no security. The company will have no benefits except direct pay for the worker. The knowledge worker is his/her own company and vacation, non-government health care costs, retirement funds, etc. will all be the responsibility of the worker.

With this independence, the work of the manager will change, but, it will still exist. From command/control, the tasks have become and will continue to be more co-ordination and inspiration based.

The individual artist often performs solo in superb fashion. So, what motivates the individual artist to perform at peak levels in the orchestra? The obvious answer is compensation. Whether you are an artist or knowledge worker, your base need is still to earn enough compensation to be fed. But after that, we can move up Maslow's hierarchy of safety, social esteem and self-actualization and find important parallels for coordinators to consider with knowledge workers. Once gathered, the workers can enhance future security as individuals, via their performance within the team. A resume that includes playing second fiddle on an enormous hit song is far more impressive than one which has the solo artist performing alone in a subway station. So, the coordinator must inspire the individual worker with the potential that exists by simply being part of an Oscar winning film, even though everyone disbands when filming is done.

This motivation of self value within team performance will include many traditional criteria but will also add an enhanced element of pride. The individual sense that contribution truly matters may be greatly enhanced when properly promoted by management. Positively reinforcing that performance by the team is crucial to the overall objective, but, performances by individuals within the team may stand on their own as value tests to be considered by future employers. Further, it should be the manager's role to point out that all current players form a bond. One of the great business tools of all time is Napoleon Hills "Think and Grow Rich." Hill's assertions related to the value of creating a circle of friends upon whom you rely for advice and connection is at the heart of what he found to be common amongst successful people.

Each new assembly of knowledge workers should know explicitly that fellow workers are the basis for future contacts, future recommendations and future work. The manager is not just motivating the worker to perform for obvious reasons at hand, rather, it is performance that will surely affect the worker as a business.

Within the same framework of worker as autonomous business, delineating the opportunity to compete should also be a managers chance to promote performance. Traditional performance reviews may be replaced by portable scorecards. It would seem that some bright entrepreneur could come up with a scoring format that might be broadly accepted as a performance reference for individuals.

When competition is reduced to the comparison of single workers, most of the confusion and concern created by the complexities of a larger organization are summarily stripped away. Using athletes for comparison, often, teams are blessed with superb players, but, just as often, poorer players get by simply because the star player has compensated for their shortcomings. How often does the batter just ahead make life easy for the one who follows that superior performance? How often does a running back excel because the prowess of the quarterback has loosened the defense. Examples abound in all team sports. However, in individual sports, the players are easily compared with competition on a clear and concise basis. The boxer, the golfer and the tennis player are each viewed as a single unit, fairly easily ranked compared to team rankings. The very context that we consider athletes likely put them in our minds first as part of the game they play. Comparatively, I think of many individual sport athletes where the player comes to mind first as an icon, then as a player of his/her sport.

When taken to a logical conclusion, my suggestion does not eliminate the human resource professional. Rather, it changes the function from practitioner to teacher. It actually elevates the value of the role because now, my friend, the mini-steel factory owner must be taught the subtleties of human resource management. While administrative recruitment functions can be delegated, he must learn to interview for technical competence and for behavioral patterns. He must learn to connect, or for the non-hires, not connect based on data and on instinct. He must learn to fall in love so that he will be willing to bet part of himself on the success of the new addition to his team. And he must learn to share his skills with people at a level that they become part of the skills of each member of his team. The other skills can certainly be supplemented by the teaching human resource professional. The difference will be like that which applies to consultants for the business. Technical expertise can be hired on an effective basis from consultants. They can set up the processes which they have effectively set up before. They can distribute information which they have garnered through education and experience. But, at the end of the consultancy, they move on to other clients. They have no significant skin in the game.

With all that is suggested above, I am not suggesting a revolt wherein HR staffs are summarily dismissed. Rather, with the vast array of tools readily available in the knowledge worker era, it is time to evolve back to an environment where responsibility for each hire once again becomes a very personal and complete connection.

Financial Management

The position of controller should entail all of the concerns of general management without concern for the effects of criticism on human resources. Serving the needs of general management with detailed analysis of the performance of capital and personnel are the objectives of the controller function.

In the old days, before management, man would reap what he sowed and sow what he reaped. Then, the crop got bigger and man hired man. You were an owner or an employee. Then, man hired the second man and instantly, controls were needed. Peter Drucker referred regularly to Frederick W. Taylor as the pioneer in the organized study of time and motion in the late nineteenth century. Frederick W. Taylor was responsive to what he considered amateurish disciplines in industry. A century after Taylor's death, he would be surprised at the depth and complexity that management has assumed and the increase in controls needed to monitor progress. Why do functions exist? How do they serve the customer?

The various functions within a business should compete for resources. The barometer for where favor should be placed is a function served by the controller. While general management may see strategic value in innovation that may be proposed anywhere within business, the controller maintains the focus on what has performed, not on what may perform.

In addition to internal performance, control functions should be data driven regarding customer and competition performance. Much of the collection of data should be by design, control functions. Analysis of data should be shared with relevant functions, especially marketing. Controls are technical and mechanical in nature and seem best suited for the skills present in the control function. Functional managers need to be trained to understand the implications of numbers so that effective decisions are enhanced by analysis and remain customer concentric.

As a team member, in my experience, the controller was always the one person in the company who could regularly be appointed "hit" person. It is important to remember that, if you happen to be the head of the company, an associate will almost always register and remember every word you share with him/her. Therefore, measured consideration of how each word will be received is critical. It is common to suggest that it takes ten positive comments to balance the weight given to one negative comment by the recipient. With that in mind, if the business had to have one person who would generally be seen as the naysayer, the negative curmudgeon, that person for my preference should be the controller. In order to assure that the controller saw that I did care about their career development, I would always take time to explain why they were cast in the role of "bad cop". I would explain how I would follow up as "good cop", but still cop, still enforcer. The important distinction was that I needed the continuing support of team members. Seeing how this method of communicating could work intimately prepared the controller for the potential that he/she could become the company head.

Accounting and the Controller functions have a very close relationship in many ways. Obviously each lives in a world of numbers. However, in many ways each is as distinct from the other as sales is to marketing.

Accounting follows specific, acceptable rules for where numbers are placed. Conventions like "first in, first out," or "last in, first out" tell us a performance story with transparent criteria. Consistent use of depreciation, amortization and accrual help level the ups and downs of cycles as we view performance. In all cases, accountants are responsible for putting the correct numbers in the appropriate columns. Like many engineering tasks, most accounting tasks are objective, not subjective. National and even international standards for what is acceptable mean that the accountant refers to and abides by rules, not the discretion of management. The discretion of management in accounting should be used to define what a "significant digit" is for the company. To list or look for pennies usually costs dollars. Anything that is not significant should not be counted or considered.

In many businesses, the accounting functions are performed by the person designated as controller. In larger companies, accounting appropriately reports to the controller who is the "general manager of numbers." The controller is as concerned about the balance of cash flow between Accounts Receivable and Accounts Payable as with the performance of a product or service resulting from research, design and innovation. Within the accounting discipline, where I have no training or experience, management generally expects accuracy so that the tools of balance sheet and income statement can be considerable. Mistakes in posting procedures can undo an entire business when stakeholders lose confidence.

Within the Age of Autonomy, tools that further enhance the applicability of generic "scorecards" should be of great value to the innovator and the customer. The all too common cry that, "my business is unique and cannot use generic tools," should be offset by tools that are not generic, rather, by tools that will be easily refit to fit the needs of each "unique" business.

Business will always include criteria that are objective and subjective. Even the creation of what we call objective involves subjective decisions. A basic problem with entrepreneurial and/or management decision making is the lack of scoring that would serve to promote decisive action.

Controllers within each industry do follow norms for determining economic health. In direct marketing, RFM stands for recency, frequency and monetary value. RFM is a qualifying way to discern the value of customers. A sale per square inch analyzes how catalog pages perform in dollars of products sold. Things like sell through rate and sales per square foot are common for retailers. Manufacturers consider finished inventory, work in process, raw materials and various measures of value added at specific points in time. In addition, the controller as the protagonist should consider, develop and maintain barometers to inform the CEO where the business is in its life expectancy.

There are unique data which should be scored on a volume basis. At Eastbay, we developed what we labeled a "Saturation Factor." In its simplest form, we wanted to understand how much growth we could expect based on demographics.

When I joined Eastby in 1992, one of my first objectives was to delineate existing customers by location with the analysis regarding possible compelling reasons they bought from us rather than through other retailers. To my surprise, only a few percent of sales came from California even though California represented 12% of U.S. population. I quickly learned that most of Eastbay's new buyers came by referral. Starting the business in Central Wisconsin, we could draw circles around the pattern of growth in sales. Kids would tell other kids about the catalog and new catalog requests were the result. This was easy to understand.

Further, it appeared that response rates, i.e., the number of orders per 100 catalogs mailed, were highest in the more rural areas of America. That too was simple to understand. If you lived in Hibbing, MN, you almost certainly saw less athletic product assortment than kids who lived in the Twin Cities.

Still further, our results selling various sports products varied wildly by state. We only needed to look at each state's level of participation by sport to see that Texas, Ohio and Michigan would outsell other states with football products simply based on the high level of participation per capita.

Response rates in general were fascinating to me. Where our average ordering rate, or as the industry termed it, percent per 100 catalogs mailed was 3.5% for our overall response, Alaska gave us a 10% response rate. It made sense that a healthy population in a state with few retailers would love to buy from catalogs. In 1992, the obvious problem was that Alaska had 550,000 people and California had 30 million people. We needed more sales from a market that had terrific retail presence based on population.

With a controller we brought in from my old employer, Apogee, we sliced and diced the numbers every way we could conceive. Our controller, John Schaefer was strong enough so that he would later serve a stint as President of Cornerstone Brands, which included Frontgate, Improvements, Garnet Hill, Territory Ahead and numerous other brands.

The key to all of the above was that controls allowed us to see where we had grown most easily. We could surmise why we had grown and where we might grow most easily in the future. Most important, we could predict when overall growth might slow. We could consider the appropriate shift from taking existing products to new markets to finding, sourcing or creating new products in order to grow our share of existing markets.

This frenzy for numbers fed our curiosity and killed any tendency toward complacency. It also tended to suggest when we might consider selling the business.

Peter Drucker always reminded us that business exists to create and retain customers. Profit is not an objective for business; it is a cost of business. Profit is the fuel that feeds future investment in existing and potential new products and services.

Whether large or small, every business should regularly schedule a review of its people and its processes. The review should be predicated on scoring scales that are objective and agreed upon in advance.

As an autonomous function, specialization of control tools may greatly enhance the quality of scrutiny. Most of what is written regarding finance has dealt with fact and the need for the Controller to serve as an antagonist within the business. In addition, scores can certainly show what may be right within the business.

The ever increasing volume of available data is opportunity and threat. More detail in data can lead to better analysis and better objective setting. It can also lead to more minutia, dissected but never used. If you do an audit of reports produced in most businesses, you are likely to find volumes of data produced on a regular basis, but never used for anything more than curiosity.

For all financial management, the budget, income statement and historic comparison are maintained as the company scorecards. Failure to maintain these scorecards will almost certainly result in missing key indicators for action. In my experience, each income statement always included three columns wherein budget, actual and prior year numbers could be compared listing the applicable changes in percentages for a very transparent review.

While income statements keep score, balance sheets indicate the health and trends in the business. Too often, when businesses are managed by the checkbook and/or income statement only, barometers of change are simply missed. Things like growth in days of inventory, days in accounts receivable or a decrease in average days in accounts payable are not seen as indicators of a decline in business performance.

As noted earlier, every line in an income statement and balance sheet should be owned by someone in the business. Similarly, every analysis should be coupled with an objective outcome and actionable steps. That is true today and should not be lost as we create the tools of an autonomous financial function.

Influencers

There are countless examples of CEO's whose approach to
business distinguished them from competition. I have studied
some and met and worked with others. My intent here is to point
to distinguishing characteristics that I have tried to remember
as I have considered appropriate strategies and objectives. Not
all are frenzied and there are various levels of success. These
are simply people with whom I had encounters with lasting
impressions. There may not be profound conclusions about each
one mentioned, but, for me there are profound memories.

The first CEO with whom I had contact was Larry Niederhofer
of Wausau Metals in my small hometown of Wausau, WI. I met
Larry when his company, Apogee Enterprises bought Wausau
Metals for $2 million in cash in 1969. I was a 17 year old part-time
shop worker at the time. Larry had served as Apogee's Controller
but, when the seller of Wausau Metals announced post-closing
that he would never come back to the business, Larry found
himself in the role of CEO. For me, after 6 years of part-time and
full time shop work and a bachelor's degree in Political Science
and History, Larry gave me a chance to train as an estimator in
this small company. At the time, of about 50 total people, only
3 of us had college degrees. What I saw in Larry was frenzy over
numbers. As a CPA, he seemed more comfortable with numbers

than with people. By age 26, Niederhofer entrusted me with the chance to run the few month old start up division, Nanik. What I learned from Larry as I managed explosive growth in this first U.S. wood venetian blind manufacturing company since the Civil War was to build controls. Niederhofer had been a classic example of inspect, don't expect. Unlike the proponents of slow, controlled growth, I came to think that any volume of growth was comfortable as long as we created tools, pulses on the business that told us with some certainty that the growth was healthy and affordable based on profit and the other entities competing for capital. For many years Larry and I worked in complementary fashion. Larry was the boss who knew that I needed to read Dale Carnegie and might benefit from reading Drucker, if I could understand Drucker. Larry understood numbers and I understood people. We both learned a little about the others expertise along the way.

At our parent company, Apogee enterprises, the founder and board chairman, Russ Baumgardner was nothing like Larry Niederhofer, Russ was an attorney who never practiced law. He was said to be one of the original directors of NASDAQ, which I guess meant he worked with Bernie Madoff. What I learned that is still compelling from Russ was trust. On numerous instances after becoming Apogee Wausau Group president at age 31, I tried to tell Russ about the opportunities and risks associated with the various divisions under my responsibility. The only question Russ would ever ask was, "if all fails, what do we salvage." In all other cases, Russ would say, "I have total faith in you, I don't need to know." It was as if he had thrown a football back over his shoulder and never looked to see if I caught it. Whether blind trust or a simple lack of interest in details, the effect was to create a compelling desire to never let him down. I learned that trust can be threatening and motivating at the same time.

These were inside CEO's who had an effect on my early vision of management. Others have been very close also, but, not in the same manner as the first view, as it is in most experiences.

Hank Johnson is only familiar to me through his book, "Corporate Dream: Making it in Big Business" (1990). While doing pro bono consulting in 1991 for my two friends Rick and Art who owned the athletic products catalog, Eastbay, I read Hank Johnson's book to grasp how he helped turn Spiegel's catalog from near bankruptcy to an icon. As a long time believer in niche market development, I always told associates that it was smarter to be special to someone than available to everyone. What Hank Johnson found at Spiegel was likely not unlike what he had managed as the head of a rather unsuccessful generalist retail chain called Arlens. Johnson also had experience at Montgomery Ward's and Avon. Spiegel's was a catalog general store offering a bit of everything to every market segment. What Johnson perceived in 1976 was the emergence of the professional female. He suggested to the nearly bankrupt company board that he could turn Spiegel's around in 5 years. The view of timing was practical. The frenzy with which Hank Johnson attacked the women's niche market was impressive. These characteristics of dedication to a market segment stayed with me after I joined Eastbay where the market segment served was the 14-24 athletes. Where Hank Johnson succeeded in occasional introductions of pricey designer apparel, Eastbay would simply need access to marque athletic shoes from Nike, Reebok, Asics and others. Unfortunately, because catalogs, especially Eastbay, were considered discounters, none of the marque product was available to my friends in 1991. But more on that later, for me, Hank Johnson represented a clear thinking merchant who provided bread and butter professional apparel for women along with tantalization fashion wear from designers like Gloria Vanderbilt. Unfortunately for Spiegel's; after Hank Johnson left the company in the mid-80's, gone too was their hold on a great niche.

Hank Johnson said that his customers became obsessions. He picked his niche and all they did at Spiegel's "flowed" from customers within that niche. His dedication was special as were Spiegel's results under his guidance.

What I will always remember is that it is important to "stick to your knitting." That does not mean you cannot take new products to existing customers or existing products to new customers; it means that your focus should not waver in a manner that you are no longer special to the primary market you serve.

While still in my role as a group President for Apogee's Wausau Group, I met a special CEO for a full day of one on one education. Having outplaced the President of our Window Coverings Group, I found myself managing four additional divisions added to the group of small architectural metals and metal finishing plants in our group. One of the window covering companies was a small franchise operations with about 100 Window Works stores. Having cut my management teeth in the window covering business, I was fine with the market and our products, it was franchising that was new and difficult for me to grasp. Through the relationships of our associates, I was able to schedule a day in August of 1991 in Stamford, Ct. with the founder and CEO of Subway, Fred DeLuca. Much about Fred DeLuca was impressive to me. On the day I met him, the most impressive things for me was that he spent the entire time with me and I was nobody in the franchising world. Our tiny franchise operation was a loser and Fred knew it. His frenzy seemed to me to be in details. I remember people popping their heads in his office with one sentence updates that might generate a few words from Fred, always with an unmistakable move of his lower lip upward. His wife was very active in the business and may have been in the office more than out. This seemed to me to be a family business. Among the various questions I posed to Fred DeLuca was why Subway had not gone public. He handed me a summary income statement that I recall as showing $102 million profit for the previous year and I understood immediately that he lived in a world unfamiliar to me. The fact that he still came to work every day and his wife and mother were there that day too seemed unreal. Fred explained that too much of his time was now spent with the legal department. He said that franchisees existed in 3 levels. One level had people who should not be in the business because they simply did not have the right commitment to work. That tier was not likely to pay royalties and very likely to sue to recover their losses. The next tier worked hard but needed attention to make them work smart on a regular basis. The third tier performed well, needed little and often wondered why they should pay royalties to a franchiser who was not needed for their continuing success. That is my recollection from a one day visit twenty years ago. Fred DeLuca was a delightful vibrant entrepreneur in a very tough business environment. The fervor he had seemed permanently engrained in his being. He helped me decide an otherwise debatable position. We soon sold Window Works and got out of the franchising business. Where Subway was a terrific franchise with a great operator, we were uncommitted, inexperienced and happy to cut our losses through a sale of the business. My sense is that I will never get involved in a franchise business again. By nature, franchise concepts are someone else's baby which franchisees are trying to adopt, raise and nurture. Except for the rare few, they are fraught with pitfalls.

Once at Eastbay the chance to encounter a few storied CEO's was a derivative of succeeding with a plan that seemed a stretch when I joined Eastbay in May of 1992.

As mentioned, when I had done free consulting for my running friends Rick and Art, the two partners who owned Eastbay, I had no intent to ever leave my position within Apogee Enterprises. Apogee was a public company and while our various divisions in Wausau, WI amounted to very little on a national scale, I was a "captain of industry" in our little town. Plus, Apogee had allowed me to run businesses since I was 26 years old.

Rick Gering and Art Juedes were born two days and two houses apart in Wausau, WI. The fact that they started a sports products business out of the trunk of a car in 1980 at nearly 28 years of age was not a surprise. The fact that they turned it into a $37 million catalog retailer by 1992 was the stuff of legends in our small town. In the years they had operated the business, neither talked about the size or status of the company. Then, they asked me if I might have time to look at the operation and give them some tips. They said that while sales were booming, profits had been flat for three straight years. Because I really liked them and because Art had been a year behind me at the same high school, I agreed to lead a planning session, not unlike what I did with most of my time at Apogee Wausau. The best part of helping Rick and Art was that they were simply good people. In different ways, they both had coaching skills that made you like them. However, behind closed doors they could not have been more different. If one said yes, the other said no! At the end of the day, they somehow compromised on most issues and continued moving forward.

In a session with the Eastbay staff, it became clear that with each new challenge related to growth, the answer was to hire a new consultant. Although the company was populated with a good home grown staff, there was more hard work than good planning accompanied by smart work and it seemed consultants were everywhere.

So, when our review and planning phase ended, I suggested to Rick and Art, that they were at a point and size where a purposeful move from the entrepreneurial to managed phase might help them to build what had become a flat bottom line in their company. In fact, based on top line growth, it was appropriate to point out that flat profit on growing sales actually meant a decline in cash on a very threatening level.

As we looked for candidates internally and externally, co-incidentally, I was told that the number of divisions I was managing at Apogee had grown bigger than my ability to handle them. In hindsight, that was true. At the time, it was a mild but motivating insult that caused me to negotiate an agreement to move to Eastbay. Although Rick and Art would not agree to parting with any common shares in their 50/50 partnership, they did offer me 25% of the profit we might make above the amount they found themselves stuck on for three straight years. Within a few months, we fired all the consultants and began to hire good talent. We doubled the profit the first year and grew profit by a third in each of the next two years. Because cash was the fuel needed to fund growth, there was no cash to pay my bonuses. At that point, there was sufficient trust to convert the debt to me into equity in the company. Based on the past success of two equal partners, I pledged to myself that I would never side with one partner over the other. In the subsequent years, every decision was made by consensus, an often laborious process. Years after joining forces, I needed Rick's and Art's Social Security numbers for a filing. When Art shared his number, I verbally repeated it without writing it down. When he asked how I remembered it I told him I would never forget it because mine was the same except that mine ended with a 6 and his ended with a 7, one behind me. While I was 10 months older in a very large population, this, added to their birthdates made it seem like things were supposed to work out for us.

The greatest threat at Eastbay was that Nike had removed the right of any cataloger to sell Air products through catalogs. When Eastbay sued Nike on what was considered a slam dunk case in which Nike had violated Wisconsin's Fair Dealership laws a few years earlier, legal bungling on the Eastbay side actually caused them to lose a case which years later, Nike's Chief General Counsel told me he was certain Nike would lose.

So, our strategy was qualitative. The key word was more. We needed more statement level products from Nike and in 1992; we were allowed to sell no statement level product, only non-Air shoes. Statement level products existed for all athletic brands. Products aligned with marque athletes and products which utilized the brands best technology were designated as "statement" level. We needed Nike to like us "more!"

One month before deciding to join Eastbay, Asics also decided to no longer sell statement product through catalog merchandizers.

That meant Eastbay would have no Asics Gel shoes, their best and biggest selling running shoes.

When we set about on our goal of getting the best of all athletic brands in our catalog, it seemed unlikely that we would ever be afforded an audience in the top executive offices of Nike, Reebok, Adidas or any other premier brand. While the strategy seemed like a long shot, our objectives were detailed and shared with any brand that would listen. We would stick with a plan to serve young athletes with respect for them and their playing goals. Rick and Art had attempted to do just that since opening Eastbay in 1980. We added the promise that we would honor the brands by avoiding early discounts on statement products tied to image programs they promoted. Of course, the problem was that no CEO would authorize our sale of their statement products.

We built campaigns with slides that showed our growth, our demographics and our promise. Most presentations were limited to local and regional sales reps who always said, "nice, but there is no chance." Then, after the 1992 draft, Nike and Reebok battled over signing the number one pick, Shaquille O'Neal, the 7'-0" phenom from LSU. When Reebok won the battle, Shaq was introduced and given plenty of promotion products. When he was presented with a super XL size Above the Rim shirt he was said to say, "I just bought that from Eastbay." We used that news to press for an audience with Reebok's President. Armed with our presentation, Rick, Art and I went to Boston to make our pitch. As we plead our case, it was obvious that the greatest interest lay in the mailing list we owned but never sold. With 3 million new 14-24 year olds asking for the Eastbay catalog each year, Reebok saw access to our multi-million name list as a gold mine in their battle to once again gain the number one position over Nike. When we turned down a $1 million offer for use of our list, they were surprised but impressed. What we did promise was that if we were allowed to sell the first Shaq shoe, we would sell them at MSRP in the catalog and give them our best location, inside cover, page 3, top of page.

When we left, we had no commitment. Soon, we learned we would be sold 200 pair with a suggested retail price I recall as $125, huge for the time. On the first weekend the Shaq shoe was available in retail stores, sales lagged because it was a "dog." It was an ugly overpriced shoe. Our catalog arrived in home the next Monday and our allotment sold out in hours and at suggested retail. Retail stores had already slashed the price before our catalogs even arrived in home. In a small way we proved that we had a great audience.

We had met Nike's regional and national sales manager but, we made little progress even though the regional sales manager was impressed with our operation. He was Mark Duggan and he would later serve as President of Nike's Bauer division. After we premiered the Shaq shoe on page 3, the sales manager of Nike, Gary DeStefano called to ask why we had made the so-so Shaq shoe look so good. The answer was simple; it was because Nike refused to sell us their statement products. The light went on for DeStefano and he assured me that we would likely build a much closer relationship based on how we now handled ourselves with statement products. He made the offer for us to visit Nike to discuss the future. After a few trips to Nike headquarters in Beaverton, OR, it seemed like no time had passed and we had a contract to be their only approved catalog Air products seller. It was a legal marketing agreement and it led to a contract where we garnered 2-5 years exclusive contracts to produce Nike catalogs. We succeeded with a strategy I had long espoused. If you want someone to want you, have them see you with someone they find attractive, or with whom they feel competitive. After losing the number one spot to Reebok in 1986, Nike did not want to see us help put Reebok back on top of the industry.

While we liked the Reebok people, we never saw Shaq as a good product icon. Many kids could dream of being Michael Jordan. It is a rare person who dreams of being 7 feet tall, 300 pounds with a size 20 shoe. The biggest ticket to success in our thinking was Nike Air.

The significance of all of this build-up is that it leads to a number of meetings with Nike founder and Chairman Phil Knight. We also got to know Nike's current CEO Mark Parker and Presidents Tom Clarke, Charlie Denson and Gary DeStefano. What struck me the first time we visited Nike is that they seemed to me more of a sports team than sports company. As time went on, I tried to compare the Nike culture with other sports companies. The team feeling in the sports world was different than in my construction industry past. However, no matter what I saw, I saw Nike was different than the others sports companies. Nike was like the Yankees in baseball or for me, the Green Bay Packers in football. In sports products, Nike is THE TEAM.

Since most people know quite a lot about Nike, suffice it to say that Phil Knight had a soft spot in his heart for Eastbay for two reasons; Eastbay, like Nike started from the trunk of a car and Eastbay, like Nike considered performance products first and foremost. Fashion products tagged along only, never as high priorities.

Before commenting on the take away from Phil Knight, comments about other key Nike players, all eventually named presidents or CEO are worthwhile.

We always told people at Nike that Mike Duggan, the Nike Regional Sales Manager in Chicago, discovered Eastbay. Remember that our strategic goal was to get more of the best products Nike offered, statement product. While Eastbay people were well liked, we were highly mistrusted. If you include consideration for the fact that brands like Nike developed product, sought and managed the factories that produced the products, hired the athletes to promote product and maintained the liability for the quality of products, all retailers exist simply as conduits to the consumer. While this small part carried little liability, retailers carried an enormous part in building and maintaining brand integrity. To digress a bit, I remember sitting in one meeting just after Nike premiered the basketball shoe aligned with NBA New Jersey Net player Keith Van Horn. While neither Van Horn nor his shoe were the subject of a meeting in Beaverton with Foot Locker executives, including me, and Nike top executives, Phil Knight stopped in to check on our progress. With an impromptu outburst, Mr. Knight screamed at our Foot Locker CEO to the effect that Nike had spent millions of dollars on product development and promotions for the Van Horn shoe and Foot Locker broke price at the launch of the product. Van Horn had been the number two overall pick in the NBA draft and obviously a sizeable investment for Nike. What I took from this outburst had twofold implications. First, I saw how the threat of retail decisions effected how brands viewed us. Second, our Foot Locker CEO, Roger Farah seemed stunned by how Nike's founder could treat his biggest customer. But, more on Roger Farah later, for now, we return to Mark Duggan's "discovery" of Eastbay and his effect on me and our business.

Mark was a New Englander like his boss and mentor Gary De Stefano, Nike's national sales manager. While our Nike reps from Minneapolis were good people, they were not Nike insiders, as mentioned earlier, Nike hierarchy felt like a team. My sense was that former athletes who played on the Nike team had greater influence than non-athletes seemed relevant with Duggan. He had been a college runner and carried a calm swagger. Duggan was exceedingly quiet but attentive. When we finally talked him into visiting our Eastbay office in Wausau, WI, from his Chicago base, we felt we might have a shot at advancing our cause. Our presentation was heavily numbers oriented. With a house list of millions of names, mostly age 14-24 we knew we owned a gold mine. Kids that age were not listed on public information lists. We pointed to the fact that when we mailed this person an Eastbay catalog, it was almost certainly the only mail with their name on it. We also showed Mark that 3 million new kids requested the catalog each year.

We showed Mark Duggan our sales of spiked and cleated shoes which proved that we were largest seller of track spikes in existence. With basketball shoes, worn mostly for fashion in the early 1990's, Mark knew that the normal shoe retailers sold a size run wherein size 10-1/2 was the top seller. At Eastbay, we showed that our top seller was size 12. Kids with size 12 shoes are more likely to actually play basketball. While all of our numbers were impressive, they did not convince Nike Beaverton executives to consider offering us any Air products immediately. We had Duggan on our side but, he could not get Nike corporate to listen. It was only after we presented the same data to Reebok, only after the release of the Shaq shoe that we caught the interest of Nike sales manager, Gary De Stefano. With Mark Duggan as our shepherd, Eastbay founders Rick, Art and I made our mission to the Nike mecca. What I saw in Mark Duggan was a quiet perseverance. What was obvious in Beaverton was that Mark was respected as a straight shooter, not flashy in his presentation but, with intellectual integrity that appeared unquestionable. While we eventually had less contact with Mark Duggan he did go on to substantially greater roles within Nike, including a stint as National Sales Manager and later as CEO of Nike's Bauer division.

The Nike campus did not feel like part of the Portland suburb of Beaverton. The Nike Campus didn't feel like any business we had ever seen. Instead of a monster high rise, the headquarters are set in a University like setting. There are exquisite gardens supplied by Japanese partners who had provided production capacity for Nike. When we arrived, we entered the welcoming center named the Pre after Oregon premier runner Steve Prefontaine. The various buildings around the campus were named for Nike athletes. The buildings are located around a large man-made lake with a restaurant nicely positioned at the edge of the water. This magnificent 200 acre collegial setting was surrounded by a berm that seemed to further the sense that what existed on the inside was unique, unto itself. In addition the berm made a nice outdoor running trail of about 2 miles.

Where Mark Duggan left an impression of quiet consistency, Gary De Stefano exemplified the consummate sales person. He exuded a charm and showed an interest in others that seemed not only consistent but genuine, not contrived. Although Gary was the U.S. National Sales Manager when we met, it was not hard to predict he would become a company President someday. Today, Gary is the Global Operations President of Nike. What I saw in De Stefano was follow up on any detail beyond anyone in the industry. Whether the resolution of an issue required a positive or negative response from Nike, Gary delivered the message. He seemed uniquely able to deliver bad news in a very positive manner. For me, it was impressive to see that this communication attention to detail was truly an exception to any executives I had seen.

When we met Nike President Tom Clarke, it seemed to me that he was an inside thinker, more product driven than people driven. Where De Stefano oozed charisma, it seemed the Tom Clarke, known on campus as TC, was considering the technical value of things, including customers. We liked TC but had little direct contact with him. During meetings wherein Nike was attempting to buy us, TC said little but seemed contemplative and analytical. After we sold Eastbay to Woolworth, later known as Venator and then simply Foot Locker, we met TC in NYC for a strategy session. I will always remember that when he asked us if we wanted to run before the meeting, our Vice President of Merchandising Dick Johnson and I agreed. When he suggested we meet outside our hotel, Marriott World Trade Center, all that was left to set was a time. TC suggested 6 a.m. When I questioned the time based on his projected flight arrival after midnight from the Pacific Time zone, he told me that he was committed to live in the time zone he was in at the moment. Dick Johnson and I met him and for me, two things were clear. TC had greater commitment than me and, like Dick Johnson; TC was too fast for me even though we were both born in 1951. The other strange remembrance was that TC wore orange Huarache racers to train. That in itself was not unusual, what was odd was that he said he liked that model so much that he had a dozen pair for future wear. Neither Dick Johnson nor I said anything while running with TC but wondered together later why Nike would not just produce more product from the same last and same upper design. After all, TC was the President. Having headed up Nike marketing but, with a definite slant toward product technology, TC was a comfortable but quiet guy. When he followed a Nike norm and took an extended sabbatical to refresh himself, TC was soon moved to other assignments after the sabbatical. All of this was very likely according to a plan embraced by all. However, from the outside it seemed strange that TC followed the protocol but was soon relegated to a lesser role. For me, the lesson was that you never step aside, even for an instant, lest you find yourself replaceable. I should have been even more attentive and inferred that you cannot step aside mentally either, my own failing which I committed at the end of my Eastbay years.

The two people on the Nike inside who seemed to assume the power positions were Charlie Denson and Mark Parker. The timelines are fuzzy for me but do not matter much regarding my observations. It seemed to me that Charlie Denson had leap-frogged over Gary De Stefano to garner the Nike Brand Presidents' role. The significant move Denson had made was to run Nike Europe, a move that seemed questionable to me at the time. I could not have been more wrong. The global experience is likely the differentiating factor that gained enough advantage for Denson to move ahead of the incredible performing De Stefano. The same gutsy move occurred at Foot Locker years after I retired. Dick Johnson had succeeded me as President/ CEO of Eastbay/Footlocker.com. When asked to run Foot Locker Europe, Dick packed his bags and his family and moved to Amsterdam. Today, Dick Johnson runs Foot Locker worldwide. The moral of the story seems to be if you want to run the whole show, you must step outside your comfort zone and go to places most people simply will not live.

Mark Parker is the current CEO of Nike, only the third person to hold that title. In our era, Mark was a very pleasant, very very quiet product designer. Mark was renowned as the key team member who was responsible for the Nike Pegasus in the early

1980's. He is also credited with visible Air in the late 1980's and the minimalist Presto products of the late 1990's. If you had asked me during any time while at Eastbay, I would never have predicted that Mark Parker would be the ultimate replacement for Phil Knight. I do honestly think I would have predicted that William Perez would fail as CEO no matter who he was, no matter what he had done prior to Nike. Perez, who joined Nike from the outside in late 2004 made it on Campus for just over one year. As Nike's second CEO to Phil Knight, my guess is that he never had a prayer of making it. Nike is a team, not a company. Nike has a playbook and that playbook works, Nike doesn't endeavor to build athletic products, Nike endeavors to build performance products. Nike doesn't just compete to win, others must lose. To embrace that from a background in a mere consumer products company that was privately owned was unlikely for Mr. Perez. As head of S.C. Johnson & Son, Mr. Perez helped run a family business. At Nike, he needed to run a very different kind of company where most team members knew the positions from grass roots he did not share. So, after only 15 months on the job, Perez left with an $8 million severance check.

In Mark Parker, Phil Knight could relax knowing that bridles would not be needed for this well-seasoned race horse.

In my two year stint attempting to start up the catalog/internet division of now defunct Footstar, Nike would once again be the key to success. While the $2 billion Footstar would fail due to accounting errors made in Texas a few years earlier, the challenge my team had was invigorating. With retailers Foot Action and Just for Feet as our brands, we attempted to break the Eastbay/Foot Locker 10 year old exclusive right to sell Nike Air products in catalog and online. Co-incidentally, Nike and Foot Locker retail had built great animosity over issues of control. In the process of building another catalog/internet team in Wausau, WI, I tried not to burn any bridges with Eastbay. Having helped build Eastbay into the top catalog/internet company in the industry, I still had great pride in that team. After all, I had negotiated the Nike exclusive agreements and served as the point person for all negotiations in the sale of the company to Woolworth, now Foot Locker. We had hired then Eastbay CEO Dick Johnson as our merchandise manager in 1992 for $52,000. Dick had been a financial modeler for local moving company, Graebel Van Lines. But, in 2002, with an expired non-compete; I wanted to create another financial win, for me and for Footstar. It seemed like a good route to pay for my second divorce.

Within Nike, it felt like my return to direct to consumer business could not have been timed better. Gary DeStefano was the US Brand President, Mark Parker and Charlie Denson were global Co-Presidents and Phil Knight was unhappy with Foot Locker. So, the first thing we were able to accomplish was access to all Nike Air products in incredible high allocations. In November, 2002 when I was invited to South Florida for a Nike meeting aimed at distancing themselves from Foot Locker, we, Foot Action looked like part and parcel of the second coming. At a banquet featuring many of America's great chefs, Mark Parker chatted with me for over an hour about Nike, Footstar and business in general. He still seemed to me to be very shy but, in my limited exposure, it was the first discussion that involved general business issues and not just the technical merits of shoe designs. When a few competitor retailers asked me how I knew Mark so well, I had to say that I didn't know him well. Mark just seemed interested in business at a new level. What I saw in Mark Parker was a career where you stick to your knitting with loyalty for the team and its mission.

With the aforementioned Nike players, for me, each is an example proving that nice guys do not have to finish last. For their ultimate boss, I guess I'm not so sure.

Phil Knight was and is the industry power player. At the time Rick, Art and I met him; Phil Knight was renowned for needing to bum cash for coffee on campus. He was said to have numerous speeding tickets in his Acura NSX licensed as Nikeman. He was reclusive except for rare meetings that really mattered. The fierce dedication to real athletes and performance enhancing products seemed to embody Mr. Knight. Retailers seemed to be a necessary evil, a threat that Nike had to tolerate not unlike the pizza shop which made a great pie only to hope that some bumbling fool delivery kid would not drop it or simply let it go cold.

Within non-branded products, value is created through a number of criteria, especially price. Brand availability is the key when producers create demand from your customer by direct exposure through various media. Think of cosmetic companies who create the formula and the aura of their brand using their own models and their own media. Within our Eastbay business, shoe brands created product, hired marque athletes and allocated the volume of product we could purchase. In particular, Nike guarded distribution of statement product with strict standards over which retailers could sell what products. So, in many cases the retailer finds that they exist only as a conduit, needing to serve the needs of the brand while serving the desires of the consumer.

At the risk of repeating the obvious, Nike and other retail brands created, produced and guaranteed products. Retailers represented and sold those products to consumers with promotions and pricing that often hurt the brands. Prior to Phil Knight, brands even had to bet on how much success each shoe would have through initial and fill-in volumes with no commitment from retailers. When I joined Eastbay in 1992, I was told that some years earlier Phil Knight had created an incentive of 10-15% off wholesale pricing for placing "futures" orders 6 months in advance of receipt, after reviewing samples. This simple advance forced retailers to share the risk of prospective sell through of products produced in Asia.

Over the years, we only met with Phil Knight a few times. Even though he had a fondness for Eastbay based on the same type of start from the trunk of Rick and Art's car, Phil Knight seemed to be the kind of CEO who looked at numbers and his own people, not at customers. For me, the most memorable encounter involved a growing interest by Nike executives to buy Eastbay. Clearly we had reached our goal of making Nike like us more. Not only did we secure a 5 year exclusive agreement to sell Air products in catalog, we also joint ventured the production of Nike only product catalogs that were being mailed to people who had filled out Nike warranty cards along with recent Nike product buyers through Eastbay. Gary De Stefano had visited us in Wausau early in 1994. Controller Bob Falcone, Chief General Counsel Lindsay Stewart and Nike's chief strategist, Andy Mooney, later to become the head of Disney consumer products, all visited Wausau on June 10, 1994. As a result, rumors of an acquisition hit industry rags with a suggested price of $70 million in cash.

When Rick, Art and I trekked to Nike's campus to further discuss the future, we were not excited about selling Eastbay but, respectful of our top supplier, so, we were all ears. With President Tom Clarke, Gary De Stefano, Mark Duggan and a host of others, we talked about the threats and opportunities posed if Nike acquired Eastbay. When Phil Knight sat in and quietly listened for an hour, we knew Nike was serious. Everyone knew we had the names, the history and location of the key athletes in America. At Eastbay, we always felt the threat that Nike could once again pull product away or at least limit availability whenever they chose to do so. We liked the people at Nike but, we also enjoyed the assortment we afforded our customers through Adidas, Asics, Reebok and others. It was with that discussion that Mr. Knight looked at me and asked if I thought Adidas and Reebok would sell to an Eastbay owned by Nike. I said that given a bit of time to find or create other direct to consumer routes, the answer was almost certainly a resounding no. With that he asked his Nike people if the $70 million number could possibly have merit for an Eastbay that would be half the size. With relief, I suggested that one of the greatest values Eastbay provided the consumer and Nike was that in 100 pages, kids could compare every product available in their sport and then buy Nike. A Nike only catalog might not even retain half the sales Nike had achieved at Eastbay. While Mr. Knight still suggested there was huge value in Eastbay's ability to produce a catalog in a tenth the time it took his staff to produce a single photo, certainly that could not be worth $70 million.

We left Nike without an offer but with a keen appreciation that Phil Knight was still very attuned to the value of a deal, even as one of the richest men in the world.

Within the shoe industry, two former Nike executives touched us briefly but with memorable effect. Rob Strasser was the former Nike marketing head tied to the creation and launch of the Jordan brand. After leaving Nike over disputes with Phil Knight, Strasser had things to prove to the world. He and product designer Peter Moore had taken their shot in a product design company called Sports, Inc. Adidas bought their fledgling company in 1993 in a simple move to make Rob Strasser President of Adidas USA with Peter Moore as Adidas' chief product designer.

Adidas America had been located in South Carolina. When Strasser took the job as head of Adidas USA, the headquarters was moved to Portland, Oregon. On our only visit there during Strasser's short tenure, Rick, Art and I were impressed to find a micro brewed tap beer available to employees in the company lunch room. What an idea! On the few occasions we met Rob Strasser, he would envelop you with bear hugs befitting his enormous size. He was a jolly giant with a passion for people and products. His sidekick was Peter Moore, an opposite in personality, quiet and observant. The beauty of the paring was that Strasser fostered an enthusiasm that was contagious. Moore had a flair for product design which resulted in the creation of the upscale Adidas Equipment line of apparel.

Sadly, late in 1993, at age 46, Strasser died while attending a company sales function at Adidas' headquarters in Germany. When Peter Moore took over Adidas America, it was all too obvious that the company flare had died with Strasser. It seemed to me to be a classic example of how important it was for the CEO to sell the story. Employees, suppliers and customers want to feel excitement, not caution.

In a sad footnote, in writing this journal, I checked on the status of various executives from my years in business. Robert Louis-Dreyfus, who was a cousin of Julia Louis-Dreyfus had served as CEO and substantial shareholder of Adidas Worldwide from 1993-2002. He died in 2009 at 63. I only met him at the FIFA World Cup Soccer Final in Paris in 1998. France won that year over Brazil. It meant Adidas won over Nike as sponsors. While my knowledge of Robert Louis-Dreyfus was almost zero, the memory of the party his company sponsored late night and into the wee hours of the morning after France won the World Cup will last a lifetime.

Some years later, Adidas would buy Reebok, the only shoe brand to actually beat Nike in the battle for the top spot in the long standing shoe wars. For Eastbay, Reebok was the proverbial date we won to garner the audience we wanted with our true target date, Nike.

Reebok USA was the creation of Paul Fireman who had secured the brand license from Reebok, United Kingdom. Reebok U.K. was the company known as the Foster Shoe Company referenced in the classic movie, Chariots of Fire. Fireman started the U.S. operation in 1979 after seeing the British shoe company at a Chicago athletic show he attended as part of his family's business. The product that put Reebok on the map in America was the Princess, a soft glove leather women's aerobic shoe. By 1986, Reebok did something no other shoe company has done since, Reebok outsold Nike. Remember that since its inception Nike has been run by athletes, competitive athletes, Paul Fireman is a terrific guy but, he is not a 4:10 miler like Phil Knight had been at the University of Oregon. When we later courted Reebok as a company eager to beat Nike, we never lost sight of well-known fact that Nike wanted to crush Reebok. So, once we won over Reebok, Nike had to want to work with us.

We met Paul Fireman a few times in our travels to Reebok's Boston headquarters. To say he was enthusiastic is an understatement. When he entered any presentation, the Reebok people seemed to smile and wince at the same time. Once in the room, it seemed likely that Fireman would jump in to finish any presentation in progress.

Because Reebok had been the first brand to trust us with statement product, we always treated them well. Conversely, just before I joined Eastbay, I joined Rick and Art for an Eastbay pitch to keep Asics' statement product with Gel technology. When Asics joined the bandwagon as the last major brand to cut off statement product from Eastbay, when our star rose throughout the industry, we paid little attention to the Asics attempts to court us.

After we sold Eastbay to Foot Locker, our stature as FootLocker.com and Eastbay grew with most brands. As President/CEO of FootLocker.com and Eastbay my world did not change much but the perception of me changed within the industry. Because I had been a Peter Drucker student and studied the works of MacGregor, Maslow and others, I was reasonably able to discuss business philosophy in a simple, understandable way. After making a few blunders in hiring key individuals, Paul Fireman was in search of a new President for Reebok. His head hunter, Stan Clayman, was his trusted ally when searching for talent. After a few calls with Stan, I was surprised to learn that Stan was actually recommending me as a candidate to be President. So, on May 19, 1998, I was flown to Boston, picked up by limo with Stan, who coached me about Paul Fireman.

My first comments to Paul Fireman were to thank him for the wonderful golf outings we had attended at his course on Cape Cod. Paul quickly jumped in to tell me he loved golf. He knew I was a runner but said athletics for him was pretty much limited to golf. During the hours we chatted, Paul's wife Phyllis called a few times regarding domestic things and their plans for that evening. I felt a bit like I was back in Fred DeLuca's office.

Since I was under contract with Foot Locker until January, 2000, I could only join Reebok if Paul made it work for Foot Locker. My knowledge of Reebok's history and recent struggles created a perspective that I thought would run counter to Paul's but, I had made enough money at Eastbay so that I only wanted a challenge which I could genuinely embrace, without filtering my positions to play for the audience. I suggested that like Spiegel, Reeboks success and ascent to the number one spot in 1986 was owing to the women's aerobics market. I remember Paul's comments seemed to suggest that his wife's opinion on the soft leather shoe was the important factor in his gambles to produce the Reebok Princess shoes. My opinion was that most things Reebok had done since 1986 were mediocre at best. The value of the Reebok name and the aura of the Union Jack which had been used by the company were not lost, they just needed to be dusted off and spruced up. The things Reebok had done in the effort to compete with Nike were in my opinion silly. The only meaningful victory Paul Fireman had won over Phil Knight was to sign Shaquille O'Neal and that proved a loss too. Nike had not wanted Shaq after he wore a Reebok leather jacket to the Nike campus according to Nike staff. Fireman had signed a giant but, who else could aspire to be a giant. On the smaller scrappier side Reebok had signed Allen Iverson and tried, with limited success to build a business around him with And One. Reebok's effort to gain an edgy side with the purchase of clothing brand Above the Rim simply diluted the edginess once attributed to Above the Rim as a brand. The Reebok pump had the aura of Nike Air but never gained general acceptance in the market.

I tried to suggest that Reebok had succeeded in the effort to entertain with athletic endorsers and hip hop personalities but, they had failed to inspire. To me, the best route forward was to go backwards. No brand had embraced the female athlete. At Eastbay, we surveyed female athletes enough to learn a major distinction from their male counterparts. Men played to win, period. Women played to play again. If attention to the detailed needs of the female athlete could become Reebok's singular focus, while company size might not equal Nike, their market could be better than Nike's or any other footwear and sports apparel brand.

Women already controlled the buying decisions in most families. I gave Paul Fireman the white paper I had written and sent to Harvard Business Review the year before, 1997. While it is trite today, 15 years ago when the internet was not yet a factor, I suggested to Paul that working women would be a bonanza for internet retailers like Reebok could become. I insert the "Internet Retail:" simply to show what my thinking about the internet was fifteen years ago.

Internet Retail/Groceries in, Garbage out

(Written and sent to HBR in 1997...not published)

It is difficult to get even the savviest of retailers to think seriously about the implications of internet commerce. But, the internet will have broad implications for A) the value of companies, B) value for the customer, C) employment opportunities, and D) new business.

The values attributed to internet stocks are, on the surface, absurd. From a lay perspective, it appears there is no way these highly valued companies can retain their market cap when measured against their actual performance. Without profit, for Amazon to maintain a market cap higher than Barnes & Noble and Boarders combined, with sales at a fraction of the combined retailers, simply is not logical. Yet, the impending shift in consumer preferences may actually justify a portion of the current premium.

Consider that marketing in its purest form is "value as perceived by the customer". What products, what services, which delivery of services, will make life better?

As we read the volumes of information available on the internet channel of commerce, it seems that the most basic consideration has yet to be discussed in any detail. While discussions of competitive forces, equipment advances, and product proliferation have been enumerated in great detail, little consideration has been given to value for the customer. Those still pessimistic about the future of internet sales point to the failure by catalog direct marketers to dominate most industries. They also suggest that home shopping was touted as a huge area of opportunity, but has failed to deliver substantially on its promise. They overlook the fact that, the limited success of these and other routes of direct to consumer commerce occurred because the seller, not the customer, has been in charge. The tables are about to turn. The highest value will be placed on control and service.

Catalog businesses often have expanded hours of service for purchasers, however, catalogs arrive in home on either the date requested by the direct marketer or determined by the postal service. If that date does not happen to be a point at which the customer needs to buy, the catalog likely becomes part of that week's garbage. Home shopping has an even greater restriction in that products are selected by a manufacturer or wholesaler, a director is in charge of timing and has input on selection, and, channel offerings may or may not be available in the prospective customer's area.

Moreover, traditional retail business exists in a limited physical area with product offerings confined by showroom and inventory storage areas. Hours of operation are determined by the individual store or applicable mall, and may not fit the needs of prospective buyers. With all avenues of delivery, timing and product selection appear to be lacking.

Conversely, internet shoppers can buy what they want, when they want it. They will have availability of pricing from anyone offering the same product. They can print out product photo, description and pricing from as many retailers as their search engines provide. Numerous sites already compare product and pricing available from various locations. Consumer shopping is only inhibited by the current lack of availability and speed of systems used to access sites. Even with slow response time, internet shopping is increasing at a rate disproportionate to any other form of commerce. This occurs at a point when slow response time and the general on-line inability to confirm availability of product exist broadly. Advances which will make inventory commitment, online, commonplace are just around the corner.

So, consider that the internet is always in your home and/or office, and you control it. You decide when to visit, what to look at, and when to buy. You will attach a huge value to being in control. As equipment advances occur, it is likely that you, the customer "in charge", will find this more convenient than a store, a catalog, or a home shopping channel. Additionally, as retailers realize that inclusion of internet sites within retail stores expands the offerings to customers, at whatever level is available in warehouses, we will see a proliferation of internet and intranet sites making every small box retailer a big box store.

For the company selling products via internet, advantage will go well beyond the immediate sale. Most historic reviews of database marketing efforts find high cost, low benefit. With internet sales, databases become the driving force for future offerings. Buying patterns in style, size, areas of interest, etc., all lead to offering new products to existing customers. And, in addition to knowing where you live, the internet database will have your e-mail address. Unlike you physical address, you email address is likely to stay with you. Instead of mailing costly, ill-timed junk mail, you will receive email specific to your interests and generally, only at your request.

"Blue light" specials with overstock products can be specifically directed to you, based on you size, brand history, and last purchase date. Relevant new product information will be communicated at the earliest date possible. Eventually, you will chat interactively about what you want, when you want it. Instead of shopping by style, you will configure what you will view by your preference. Customer follow up files traditionally used by progressive retailers will look like ancient history.

Beyond impact on traditional customers, internet sellers will immediately open to a global market. Used as indicators of interest, international results should lead to better focus on where future opportunity exists for a physical presence.

The convergence of television at speeds currently unattainable on PC's likely is the single most significant event in the development of electronic commerce. A shopping icon will appear on your television which provides an opportunity to buy a relevant or related product. Buy the CD that relates to the music video you are watching, download the video that relates to the song from the soundtrack you are hearing, buy the player's gloves, shoes, etc., get your championship hat or tee right now, using the "gotta have it" button on your remote control.

Speaking of "gotta have it"; it is reasonable to study consumer history as we consider the future. As the Japanese advanced production processes for transistor radios, they estimated that their own country would have a limited appetite, based on product pricing. What they failed to estimate was the "in style" factor that impacted the Japanese consumer. While disposable income was not such that large volumes of Japanese consumers should have demanded transistors, the desire to be voguish created a demand many times the projection of Japanese manufacturers. It is likely with internet commerce, that chatter will cause demand beyond any current expectations. The "must be on the in" syndrome, coupled with the increased speed of information transfer will likely be key success factors.

Does all this mean retail, as we know it, will be destroyed? No. Does it mean catalog sales will plummet? Unlikely. What it means is that internet shopping will bite into current channels. Three to five years from now that should mean 10% or so of consumer business will be done via computer or computer assisted televisions. It means that if you are not positioned to be part of the opportunity side of this equation, you will likely be a victim of the threat.

With a structural change in behavior on the horizon, those commerce companies who are first in their industry segment will garner the greatest rewards. Key first factors include:

- Companies capable of leading the customer in a friendly manner through a site designed for commerce. While games are fun, average time per visit is actually longer on commerce sites than on marketing/game sites.
- Companies first to build order friendly systems so customers can confirm availability while they are on-line.
- Companies first to use their physical locations to promote e-commerce. On-site intranet portals are a win-win from an educational and commerce perspective. Simple use of banners, ad tags and handouts enhance the impact on consumers'

consciousness. The more varied the options, the greater the perception of control by the customers.

- Companies first to offer a shopping experience will create the comfort of familiarity that is generated through the various simple steps needed to place and close an order. This loyalty is a key that every seller will race to win. And by the way, manufacturers selling direct will fail more often than succeed as they attempt to sell direct. Their basic shortcoming will be in service to the retail consumer. Their customers have traditionally been businesses, not individuals. It will take them years to build an effective, customer service driven function.

- Companies that first establish agreements with highway owners (Yahoo, AOL, etc.) enjoy the best rates and first and most effective image in the eyes of online viewers. While none of us suggests that banner presence creates a click through rate adequate to pay the highway fee, the awareness factor is important in the early stages of development.

- Companies first to utilize the increased value of their currency to enhance competitive stature. If Amazon has made any mistake, it appears from the outside to be a failure to extend control through relationship building. While key relationships exist with highway owners, valuable currency has not been used with authors and publishers to develop exclusive or restrictive relationships with regard to current and future products. The companies that endeavor to control major segments of their supply chain through private label products and restrictive relationships stand to keep customers longer.

The word commerce differentiates internet players. Highway owners exist to drive customers to directories in order to make the trip easier. While they enjoyed incredible stock prices, based on sales, it is questionable whether their long term value will retain such lofty heights. Their purpose is not unlike a physical highway. While the highway takes you from point A to point B, it is not likely that you will jump off at every roadside billboard to shop. Therefore, once the consumer learns to maneuver without these crutches, shoppers will jump immediately, through bookmarks, to their destinations. Highway values are likely to be the first to decline.

Content providers give us information of value. Whether weather, news or sports, we can get detailed data that is informative and educational. However, because links to commerce will likely fail, the value will be based on advertising dollars, not commerce. Consider that mail order companies are fortunate to get three out of one hundred potential consumers to buy. The content viewer is unlikely to link to a commerce site simply because the product offering is somehow related. If there was no initial intent to shop, most people online, being a bit more intelligent than average, will not buy. Therefore, content providers are likely to have the same value attributable to media companies, no more.

e-commerce players who have built value based solely on market share will be found out. There will however be solid performers, building e-commerce models that require sales growth, profitability and positive cash flow, and good service to the customer. Category killers will kill whole segments. However, savvy producers will become fierce in their control of distribution of product. They will likely reserve most products for themselves.

Put all this together and the stock price premiums paid for internet savvy commerce companies' competence becomes a bit more palatable. How long will the premium last? Who knows, but the first to sell and service well are likely to keep the premium longest.

In the not too distant future, there will be no need for product distributors, retail locations, or a sales force outside the location of the source for the product. In commerce, only those companies who control substance, i.e., that which requires no cause to exist in effect, have long term promise. This will mean yet another structural change in the world economy. Having moved from an agrarian economy where hoards of people moved to cities for employment, there will be little need for concentrated population with regard to the functions that run the business in the coming "click" society. With advances in technology, it is likely that management will move from a facilitation function to a consolidation of experts.

Wipe out entire tiers of employment and we are likely to see unrest. Taken to the negative extreme, there can be ugly repercussions. However, on the positive side, the facilitation of effective communication and distribution should result in shortened workweeks and higher pay at almost every level.

The major foreseeable difference in a world dominated by e-commerce is that initially it will be reactive rather than proactive. The human touch that enhances the desire to buy will be eliminated.

On the opportunity side, everything that is ordered must be delivered. Currently, there are but a few select players with delivery systems capable of satisfying consumer needs. As changes in volume occur, the opportunity for new players will abound. Obvious opportunities should exist for anyone who currently has a business that serves residences. While there are few milk carriers left, there are still the garbage collectors who must appear at least once a week to take away the remnants of last week's purchases. While uncanny today, it is not absurd to consider that the equipment used to pick up the garbage will be revamped so that it can also deliver the groceries (i.e. groceries in, garbage out).

Harry Colcord
May, 1997

With my Reebok interview, I felt I connected. It seemed to me that the company needed to reset its focus. Frankly, it seemed to me that Paul Fireman, even with his immense success was not completely comfortable in his own skin. When I compared him in my own mind with Phil Knight and key Nike people, Paul seemed to be very engaged in the effort to make the business a success. It was almost as if, because his family had been in the sports business, he was in the sports business, hell bent to do very well. This was his vocation. At Nike, the vocation seemed to inherently tie to their avocations.

As I left Mr. Fireman's office for the waiting limo, Don Hasselbeck caught up with me in the lobby. Don is a 6'-7" former NFL tight end who spent most of his career with the New England Patriots. He is also dad to Matt and Tim Hasselbeck. On that day, Don said the rumor around Reebok was that I was a candidate for the top job. He said that from what he had seen and heard of my style at Eastbay, I would be a welcome addition. I only knew Don Hasselbeck in his capacity as head of Reebok Football. I was always impressed that he came off simply as a good man, not prone to dwell on his NFL career, more interested in what was on the horizon with people, not in his past. I didn't have the heart to tell him that if I was hired at Reebok, there would be no football products.

The follow up calls from Stan Clayman seemed positive. There were a few additional questions and a summary letter I sent to Paul Fireman. When I received the following letter from Fireman, I was not surprised, but I was disappointed.

Reebok

June 9, 1998

Mr. Harry Colcord
1000 Easthill Drive
Wausua, Wisconsin 54403

Dear Harry,

Meeting you here in Boston was a true pleasure and getting to know you and what you stand for rejuvenates my hopes for the retail world. I did receive your letter, and it does present possibilities as to why I should take a risk on you for the job as President of Reebok; and I am attracted by your character and your understanding of our business and its culture.

Unfortunately, Reebok has been weakened by some poor choices that we have made in management over the past five years. We are beginning to solidify both our management, products and marketing. We are still perceived weak and lacking the outside confidence of both the retail world and Wall St.

Therefore, Harry, I do not believe that your background is strong enough nor global enough for me to provide this opportunity to you at this time. It well might be that I should take the gamble but I think the circumstances would overwhelmingly cancel both my vote and yours from the job markets. If you have an interest in approaching a different entry spot at Reebok and have the time to provide us a demonstration of your leadership, I would be most happy to talk to you about such an opportunity. I recognize this as less than your expectations at this moment, but sometimes the end result is served best by some deviation to the set plan.

If it doesn't work for us to be together, please know I have really enjoyed meeting you, and I respect your competence and your successes. At the very least, please take a bigger position at Woolworth Group and help change their weak and chaotic organization. Look forward to hearing from you.

Regards,

Paul Fireman

Reebok International Ltd. 100 Technology Center Drive, Stoughton, MA 02072 USA Tel 781-401-5000

Sometime later our board chairman Roger Farah heard rumor of my recruitment by Reebok. He said he would never have allowed it to occur and might have cut Reebok out of Foot Locker. I countered by suggesting it was likely all curiosity and never would have gone anywhere. If it ever had worked out, I suggested to Roger that it could have been a classic win-win wherein I truly understood retail needs and felt that I could soften a brand's intensity.

I don't recall the dates but, a few years after interviewing at Reebok, they hired Jay Margolis as President. I thought that because Jay had run Esprit and had stints at Hilfiger and Liz Claiborne that Paul Fireman must be buying into the need to get away from the mess they had created as a male oriented multi-sport brand and would be returning to the women's market I thought they could own, but, alas Margolis only lasted a few years and I don't know that the focus ever changed.

In 2006, Reebok sold to Adidas ending Paul Fireman's years in athletic work. Almost in irony, an old Eastbay friend from Adidas, Uli Becker is now head of Reebok. Fireman was a classic entrepreneur who saw an opportunity and pounced on it with terrific timing and great success. While the business was what he did, and did quite well, it was not who he was, it was not the fabric of his being from my limited exposure.

Not far from Reebok in physical location is New Balance, a privately held company owned by Jim Davis and his wife Anne. While close in proximity, Davis could not be farther apart from Paul Fireman in his approach to business. New Balance seemed committed to make great products for the more stable middle aged customer who didn't want change and didn't want flash. Very expensive grey shoes built on the same last, year after year did not make New Balance a big hit with our 14-24 year old customers except for rare stints where European youth felt they had discovered something "new". Because we liked Jim Davis and his people so much, we tried to convince them that a change in their logo aimed at our market might garner good results. When they sold us special make-up shoes with an elongated N, we sold them like hot cakes. When they played with a small nb logo, we were very excited. But, in the end, Jim Davis vetoed all such efforts to modify the big N logo in any way and in the end, he was and is right. In the classic dedication to niche marketing, Jim Davis had his baby aimed at a segment of the market he trusted. He tried new things like dress shoes built on running shoe lasts and NB produced limited sports apparel but only as window dressing, not as core. New Balance never got into the battles over celebrity sports figures. Instead, Jim Davis stayed committed to building more of his athletic shoes in America than anyone in the industry. All of our business with New Balance was good business. The reason it was never destined to be huge business was simple, our customers were nowhere in Jim Davis' target market. His targets were our customers' parents and he has served them very well.

Japan was an economic boom country in the late 80's and early 90's. At Eastbay, we saw a strange increase in demand for U.S. athletic brands, made in Japan. While orders originated in various places in Japan, Sony quickly grew to be our number one source for orders from Japan. In tiny Wausau, WI, we had limited ability to hire Japanese speaking operators, there simply were few available. The hours in demand presented an even greater challenge. But, a bit at a time, Japan came to represent 10% of our total Eastbay business in 1996.

As Eastbay's President, I felt it incumbent to learn more about the nature and reason for our growing volume of business. Luckily, we were able to hire at Japanese American as our International Sales Manager in 1995. When we traveled to Tokyo, our main agenda was to learn more about Sony's agenda for us.

On March 29, 1996 we met Mr. Kawano at Sony's headquarters. I expected that we would be meeting a mid-level manager, assigned to manage Sony's strange direct to consumer business.

Instead, we learned that Mr. Kawano had vacated his role as President of Sony Europe to run this fledgling catalog business consisting of Eastbay, Victoria's Secret and a dozen or so other catalogs. The first obvious question for Mr. Kawano was why? To my surprise, Mr. Kawano said that Mr. Morita, the co-founder of Sony had suggested a few years earlier that consumers would buy most products on a direct basis in the future. Mr. Kawano saw this small telephone order entry business as Sony's way to learn the business. Mr. Morita had suffered a stroke and retired two years before my visit, but, his vision still was having an impact on the giant Sony Corporation. Mr. Morita's various visions including always building smaller and better Sony products must have envisioned the changes a wired world would experience.

When I asked Mr. Kawano how Eastbay made the list of catalogs represented by Sony, I expected some detail on researching our capabilities. Instead, Mr. Kawano said that he had played baseball in his youth in Japan and he saw the Eastbay catalog had Rawlings gloves, so, he knew he had to include us. So, it turned out that 10% of our business had come to us by chance, by the luck of having Rawlings gloves.

While Mr. Morita made mistakes like failing to license Betamax, he had a vision for his 50 year old company that kept it a behemoth. Much of that success seems to have passed with Mr. Morita's passing.

I expected my commentary on CEO's would be brief and limited. The reality is that in forming my own career as a CEO, the influences upon reflection are far more pervasive for me. While I intend to summarize with my own perspective, a few more observations are relevant.

Roger Farah is the incredibly successful President and COO of Polo Ralph Lauren. From January, 1997 to August 1999, I knew him as the boss.

Had it not been for the fact that Roger's teenage son thought it was cool that his dad knew of Eastbay, we may never have been sought out by Foot Locker as an acquisition target. Roger Farah had already achieved retailing success at Rich's and Federated before assuming the reins at then Woolworth in 1994. While Woolworth struggled for years before and after Roger arrived, its Foot Locker division was the top athletic footwear retailer in America. I had met the Foot Locker division President Bill DeVries at a footwear conference where I was asked to address the conference on direct marketing. While retailers disdained the ease by which customers could look at shoes in their stores and then call to order them from our catalog, I nonetheless tried to engage them in options to sell direct. DeVries made it clear that Foot Locker had an interest in acquiring us. But, because our intent was to take Eastbay public, we downplayed Foot Lockers interest throughout Eastbay. Although we did listen to one final pitch on September 21, 1995 at a dinner DeVries hosted in New York at Spark's Steakhouse, we went public in an IPO a week later. That did not stop contact and soon Woolworth's chief negotiator, Jeff Branman was calling me. Jeff had once worked for Gilbert Harrison at Financo. Harrison had visited Eastbay with then Melville Executive Vice President Jerry Politzer proving to me that New York retailing was a very small world. While Branman was renowned as a liquidator of troubled businesses, he was a rather transparent negotiator. When Branman insisted on not negotiating through our bankers at R.W. Baird, it opened up a fun chapter in my business life where I negotiated the sale of our small public company Eastbay (symbol EBAY) to Woolworth (symbol Z…a DOW original firm).

With a $15 per share Initial Public Offering price, Eastbay opened at $19.25, proving that our 77 presentations to the investment community had been successful. Although we met our profit projections post-IPO, the stock price settled back at $15 for most of our short life as a public company, EBAY. When we did sell to Woolworth, we opened up the EBAY mark for another company which followed in much bigger fashion.

At $15, I had suggested to majority shareholders and my senior partners Rick Gering and Art Juedes that anything less than a 33% premium to our average share price of $15 would be unacceptable. Since three of us controlled over 60% of the outstanding shares, we only needed to be fair to outsider shareholders, not beholding to them to garner their votes of support.

From the onset, I think Branman considered me a naïve negotiator. In many ways, I am sure he was correct. Behind the scenes I did get good counsel from the people at Baird. While Woolworth insisted I agree to a 3 year contract, the valuation of the company could be sliced and diced many ways. As Branman anxiously and even angrily tried to educate and convince me, I grew more and more confident that he had been assigned to get this deal done, period. On Thanksgiving Day, 1996, Branman called my house numerous times to questions why I would not agree to a $19 per share purchase price. I would in turn call my nervous partners to suggest we hold out for more. Rick Gering truly did not care if we ever sold, he loved our work. Art Juedes just wanted to deal done in order to be secure for life after seeing the ups and downs of being public.

I finally suggested to Branman that because we had only been public for a short time, we thought it fair to pay outside shareholders more than the three of us would be paid. I suggested that outsiders should receive $24 a share and Rick, Art and I would take $22 at closing and a $2 per share "claw back" if we met the goals we promised to meet as part of our negotiation. When Branman started screaming at me, I remembered a recommendation from a negotiation book I had read years earlier. To win you must be prepared to walk away, truly prepared. As Branman ranted, I hung up. Over the next hour or so, I let his calls go to voicemail. Finally, when his voicemails calmed, I returned his call to say we simply did not need to sell our new public company at anything less than I had suggested. He reluctantly agreed contingent on my promise that we would not ask for anything more.

The odd part of what followed for me was probably predictable for a more experienced mergers and acquisitions person. Foot Locker endeavored to change everything about us. I kept asking Foot Locker's Bill DeVries why they had paid $90 million in goodwill on a $142 million purchase price only to ignore the goodwill associated with our way of operating. Eventually, Roger Farah outplaced DeVries and our world settled down.

In Roger Farah there was an appetite for detail I had never seen before or since. He would gather about 40 of us in a conference setting each quarter to review products and plans. People from Woolworth's might show new candy displays. People from Afterthoughts would show the newest in earrings and other jewelry trinkets. With many diverse divisions, the presentations went on and on for two days. If someone had missed a sales opportunity by under-buying products, Roger would take them apart in humiliating fashion. When one Foot Locker president tried to explain how his buyers had missed the chance to cash in on the fashion craze for tear-away nylon pants, Roger nearly brought him to tears.

Luckily, when we sold Eastbay, Roger suggested that I had earned enough "screw you money" so that he treated me very well. I soon came to see Roger as sincerely and intensely interested in building a great company. He had come from a retail background where brands fought for and even paid for shelf space. He seemed astonished by how badly shoe companies treated retailers.

Eastbay gave Foot Locker direct marketing routes to consumers that no other shoe retailer could match. Roger Farah wanted more. We met during the Super Bowl in San Diego to discuss Foot Locker's options. Struggles at the Sports Authority made acquisition of the diversified products big box chain a natural. It would make us the only retailer who controlled specialty and big box stores along with catalog and internet sales. Personally, I was happy to have gained Roger's confidence. Although he suggested my greatest value was in understanding marketing, it was satisfying enough for me.

Roger carried himself well but, the confidence was regularly disturbed by the brands. The Sports Authority deal was ill timed and never came to fruition. We did continue as Nike's only catalog approved Air products seller and continued producing Nike catalogs. We also negotiated the catalog and internet rights to be NFL Shop catalog and NFL Shop.com. A few years earlier, before being acquired we had helped Bob O'Keefe of Sports Illustrated get out of the NFL catalog business in which SI had lost money. When Bob O'Keefe ended up running direct marketing at the NFL, it only helped Eastbay get a new deal there. I thought these were high profile successes that would help us and help Roger's view of the company. Only Roger can explain why he left the company in August, 1999. For me, on one trip we had taken to Nike, Phil Knight never stopped by to greet our board chairman, his number one customer. I surmised that the sense that this industry had shifted Roger to the role of seller when he thought he was a buyer was just too distasteful.

Roger's successor, Dale HIlpert he was an operations guy. His claim to fame was that he grouped shoes by size in building Payless Shoes. As CEO of Foot Locker, I was not inspired enough to accept his offer to move to New York and felt that retirement at age 48 was better than serving a master for whom you had little respect.

Shortly after retiring and just before a photographic safari to South Africa, Korn Ferry of Miami called me with an opportunity that seemed intriguing. In that opportunity, I met Virgilio Degiovanni of Milan, Italy, along with the founder of internet retailer, Addashop. Degiovanni had made millions in Italy by launching an internet television top receiver company. He was a small, balding but debonair type who was intriguing. Thomas Corneluis was the German who founded Addashop. We met in South Beach, on

Ocean Drive at Pelican restaurant which Virgilio said was owned by his friend, the owner of Diesel jeans from this hometown of Milan.

For me, what was intriguing was that until that time I had run factories and direct marketing companies with real products and real sales. For Virgilio, real didn't mean much, it was perception that was of value. So, after a quick review of Korn Ferry's reference check and an hour of chat, Virgilio offered me $5 million, a decent annual salary and living expenses in Miami. The $5 million was predicated on taking the company public within one year of our first meeting, that day. This was early 2000 and the go go dot com boom was in high gear. I said yes but only if I could start for a few weeks and then leave for 3 weeks, to take my planned trip to South Africa. Virgilio agreed but did so in disgust. In broken English he said, "I think I'm hiring a smart CEO but already you turn a 52 week year into 49 weeks. I dunno. The $5 million bonus is for 1 year starting now!" Within 2 months of starting, our dot com boomer became a dot com bust. Our value according to a young Wassertein Perella hot shot had been $100 million one week in March 2000 and a $1 million one week later.

I only met with Virgilio a few times once we made a deal. What I saw in him was raw enthusiasm, a sense that everything was for the taking when you grab for it. I understood that Virgilio was not a favorite of Italian Prime Minister Silvio Berlusconi. After his Freedomland internet business cost investors 90% of their 300 million euro investment, Virgilio actually did 10 months of jail time. I'm not sure that the following Korn Ferry Assessment of me is real but, if it was how I was seen in the industry I worked, I could not have been more proud and humbled. I have not included it to toot my horn but rather to show that you can be seen as effective, personable and still tough minded. I suggest that the key for you, my sons, is to control appropriate emotions in various settings. It does mean you can use the entire spectrum of emotions, it means that whatever you do in business, you do with forethought, on purpose.

CONFIDENTIAL REFERENCES

These individuals have provided useful reference information regarding Harry Colcord, candidate for CEO of addΛshop.com

References

Mark Duggan
Director of Sales
Nike Corp.
503-671-4570

Duggan has known Harry Colcord for eight or nine years. East Bay was a customer of Nike. Harry and Mark put together a strategic partnership between Nike and East Bay. Duggan continued to work with Harry after East Bay was acquired by Venator.

Fred Kasten
Chairman
Robert W. Baird & Co.
414-765-3616

Robert W. Baird was the underwriter of the East Bay IPO. But also, Kasten has known Harry for 15-20 years through their mutual participation in the Young President's Organization.

Robert Nagel
Senior Vice President
Adidas
503-797-4417

Nagel has known Colcord for six or seven years while Harry was at East Bay and at Venator. East Bay is a significant customer of Adidas and Nagel worked with Harry on marketing campaigns to increase Adidas sales through East Bay.

2

Robert O'Keefe
Director of Marketing
National Football League
212-450-2664

Prior to joining the NFL about a year ago, O'Keefe was with Sports Illustrated for 8 years. About four years ago, O'Keefe was charged by SI to start a catalog and e-commerce business. He worked with Harry to develop a partnership to implement that strategy. Ultimately, SI outsourced their e-commerce solution to East Bay.

Brant Rupple
Managing Director
Robert W. Baird
414-765-3500

Brant was the lead manager on East Bay's public offering and secondary offering.

About Harry Colcord

All of the references contacted confirmed by their observations the very significant contribution Harry made to the success of East Bay. Harry was brought in by the founders of that company when they recognized the need to bring in professional management in order to grow the company and take it public. Harry did that very successfully. He adapted well, complemented the existing management team and built the company into a profitable, well run enterprise. He was able to come into the company, work with the founders and assume a leadership position without overstepping his bounds. He dealt with everyone, especially the founders, with a great deal of sensitivity, grace and respect. He honored the founders, even though Harry was far more sophisticated than they were.

The businesses that Harry had to oversee and manage were fairly complex. The company had many product groups, some of which were fairly unique in nature. In apparel and sporting goods, Harry is more of a visionary than any other retailer in the business. While Harry did not have a strong background in retailing prior to East Bay, he is an extremely quick study and is now regarded as among the most knowledgeable in the business. Harry was among the first of the catalog retailers with a significant "e" strategy. He has always thought in terms of using technology to be more effective and he understood what the use of technology could do for East Bay. Harry's knowledge of retail, systems, customer service and fulfillment are excellent.

In addition to being a visionary, Harry's execution is extremely effective. His ability to organize customer service and an excellent call center is one of the reasons that East Bay was able to grow

3

as quickly as it did. East Bay's call center grew from 200 to between 1200 and 1500 during Harry's tenure. His operations background is excellent.

In addition to knowing how to run a retail company from the operations side, Harry is also very familiar with the financial markets. He has handled relationships with the investment community very well. He did not oversell the company and always delivered as promised. Consequently, he has very good credibility within the investment community.

Harry's leadership skills are "at the top of the list" He developed strong relationships at every level and built an excellent team based on those strong relationships. He is able to attract the very best people and retain them. He is a very good communicator and listens very effectively. He is particularly good at communicating a vision and a direction and then empowering people to do whatever it takes to get the job done. Harry stays the course once the vision is articulated. He was very popular with his people, knew all their names and was greeted by his first name wherever he went in the company even after it had grown tremendously.

One of Harry's greatest assets is his ability to do a log of things at once and do them very well. He is extremely well organized. Harry is unique in his ability to very efficiently run a business because he invests nicely in the appropriate people in the right jobs. Consequently, there are no excess people and the job is done right the first time. This clearly contributed to the success of East Bay because of its reputation for excellent customer service.

Colcord is a tough negotiator. While he is always professional and pleasant, he is strong and firm. One reference said that he is like a "velvet hammer" and is tough as nails. Yet, because he is so good to work with, vendors went out of their way to include him for any special promotional opportunities. They would usually go to Harry first because he understood the business so well and was so supportive of the vendors.

Overall Harry is a real quality person. He is very easy to get along with and like. He has always tried to learn from others and is very open and honest. Despite his accomplishments, Harry has always had his ego under control. Harry is driven to succeed. He is a very hard worker and drives himself hard but manages stress very well. His integrity is unquestioned. Additionally, Harry seems able to work very effectively in many different environments. While he was very successful in the entrepreneurial environment, he adapted very well after the sale to Venator and is very well respect by the management of Venator who wanted to retain Harry.

4

I mentioned the African photo safari I took in March of 2000. The trip was called a "University" within the Young Presidents Organization in which I had been a member since 1986. Within YPO, I met many wonderful and talented people. One such person I met was a very quiet Nigerian bank President from Lagos and part of a couple I only knew as Dudan and Atedo. Atedo was the ever quiet partner while his wife Dudan was the outgoing gorgeous woman who donned tribal apparel as if in a pageant. Having spent numerous days and evenings around Atedo, I have never heard him say anything but hello and good-bye. I assumed he ran a family bank and just had little to offer. On a night when couples were debating how to raise children, Atedo finally interjected a comment. He said, "Before a child is 6, he or she can know what they want but, they cannot reason why they cannot have what they want." With that he again fell silent. Later, when Atedo and I stood alone I asked why he finally had spoken. He said with 6 children he felt he had something to offer. I said he seemed quite articulate. His response was that he chose not to talk much because his nature was such that he did not learn anything while he was speaking. When I pressed further, surprised by his demeanor, I asked if he had been educated in Nigeria. Atedo said he had earned his undergraduate degree at Harvard and his masters from Yale. For me, it was an "aha" moment. But, I will comment more on how we each learn later in the Summary.

In March of 2000 our YPO group of about 50 attendees got to spend more than an hour with Nelson Mandela (Madiba) in a tent set up at the University in Capetown. One cannot help but be in awe of such an incredible figure. After Mandela pitched us on the value of partnering businesses in his country, he took questions from our group. Two of his answers were very impressive. When asked by one of our lovely female attendees what he would choose if granted a single wish, Mandela gazed across the room. After a few seconds he smiled and commented on how many beautiful women were in attendance. He said, "In my father's time, a man could have three wives." We all laughed at his humanness.

Another questioner asked President Mandela to compare himself to Martin Luther King. To this, Mandela forcefully reminded us that Dr. King had tried to get 90% of his countrymen to recognize 10%. He said there was no comparison at all in that his life was dedicated to keeping 90% of his countrymen from destroying the 10% of South Africa's population who had controlled the wealth. He has obviously succeeded.

I'm certain I have missed other leaders my sons have heard me mention, for that I am sorry. My comments regarding my own views as a CEO are inconclusive because they come from the inside. The really important perspective on any CEO comes from scores on the outside, from associates, customers, suppliers and investors.

While I don't think he ever ran a business of any kind, the person who had the greatest influence on how I thought as a manager was Peter Drucker. Certainly other writers and thinkers had profound influences; Abraham Maslow had a very special way of seeing humankind. W. Edwards Deming had the disciplined analytic tools to change a nation. The various writings of numerous CEO's left impressions I tried to follow, not the least of which is to follow your instincts, as they are usually your best gauge.

Dr. Drucker is likely or should be mentor to more business people than anyone who ever lived. So, my claim to having studied his works, especially when so often I found myself in trouble is not novel. Unlike so many of his followers, I never even saw Drucker in person. Comically, toward the end of my career, when I could finally afford it, I did intend to attend a Drucker seminar just so I could feel I had seen the master. When I called Clairmont College, I asked for anyone who might be scheduling attendees for the next Drucker seminar.

The receptionist said the college did not schedule for Dr. Drucker but she had a number I could call. When I immediately called, the greeter, to my complete amazement said, "Peter Drucker." As I stammered through my single question, I perspired as if I was in the presence of someone bigger than life. Dr. Drucker explained that he no longer did seminars in person, only by remote feed. I thanked him without further comment feeling it would be wrong for me to take more than a minute of what had become such precious time.

Peter Drucker (1909-2005) has been written about on so many levels that it would seem foolish for me to try to add much to the litany of existing tributes. For me, Drucker was a reference book for any business issue I faced and I faced many. Drucker deduced great observations as the classic "bystander." What I appreciated most and have laced throughout most things I think and write were the questions Drucker asked. The questions of why, why, why impressed me most. As mild mannered as Drucker appeared, beginning with "Concept of the Corporation," he never stopped asking questions.

I once bought a multi-cassette taping of a Drucker seminar in a classroom setting. Unlike many of my contemporaries who also followed Drucker, I felt very comfortable with his use of terms and the tempo of his presentations. For me, Drucker looked at facts and concluded, if this, then that. His conclusions always seemed very crisp.

It seemed to me in reading Drucker's assessment of his life that money was of little consequence. When he left banking soon after he started, he said he didn't care for it and did not want to work simply to die the richest man in the cemetery. When you remove contaminants like money, you eliminate a communications filter and integrity is enhanced. The very fact that a 90 year old man still answered inquiry phone calls suggests that Dr. Drucker was still curious, still interested in what a connection might teach him about the world.

It seemed to me that Peter Drucker imagined things would evolve in better fashion if he relentlessly asked what and why. What is the task? Why do it all? What is value? To whom is it valuable?

As Dr. Drucker considered the value of man, he espoused a high Theory Y perspective. When Abraham Maslow took him to task for thinking that some individuals needed control in order to function, Drucker acquiesced, aware that Maslow was the master of human psychology. It taught me that theories about human nature like X & Y, are only theories. The varied nature of nature is seen infinitely in human nature. Appropriate treatment will always and only be a guess. The individual, the circumstances and the options will change constantly.

Reading Drucker always caused me to ask, what is productive labor? I came to see productive labor as labor that eliminates labor while continuously increasing and improving output. In the age of autonomy, how do we measure productive labor? Who measures it? How is it valued? How is it rewarded? In the old world of business, fear was in fact a sometimes needed productive tool. An otherwise uncontrolled mind can go "rapid fire" toward destructive behavior without control. Who will administer such needed control in the age of autonomy?

Sadly, Dr. Drucker leaves a likely void that will be difficult to fill. While people like Tom Peters and Jim Collins do have the curiosity about companies shown in their works, none of the current observers seem to have the depth of curiosity and the pure joy in work that Dr. Drucker showed. We are all mere mathematicians and Drucker was Einstein.

With the various people discussed there is a wide variety of experience and perspectives. As noted earlier, if there is any value in my perspective, it will be judged from the outside. For my sons what follows are comments on my management perspective, derived from my own studies, observations and experiences.

The strategic and operating planning outline in the chapter on CEO still holds water for me. It is derived from Drucker questions and expanded by simple experiences. My advice and comments for those assuming company reins are in addition to the basic advice that you follow a plan, my plan, your plan, any plan.

Before taking any major actions unless hemorrhaging, a period of assessment is important. Taking time to get to know people, associates, suppliers and customers is a critical foundation building step. This process, inclusive of assessing products and services may take up to six months.

It would be naïve to assume that major political games are not part of every company. In the assessment process, as you gauge people, are they focused on customer and product issues or are they focused on issues related to themselves and others in the company. As in an initial interview, assessing behavior patterns will be very helpful. Who is allied with whom? Where are battle lines, no matter how subtle, already drawn.

When you decide what is needed, moves should be comprehensive. Piece-mealing a plan can only cause unrest and a reduction in focus on the work to be done. You must execute.

In the age where autonomy in functions eliminates some tasks within the business forever, the assessment period is the point at which review, discussion and agreement or decisions are made so that team members know with some certainty which positions will be linked internally and which will be filled on an as needed basis.

While companies as we know them today will not disappear, they will slowly deconstruct. For the top manager, it will be important to foster a new sense of connection. Autonomy will breed a sense of fraternity versus affinity. Fraternal connections will likely require a new consciousness about what keeps people coming back together when the links are less and less sticky.

Autonomy in functions will likely make obsolete consultants as traditionally known and used. While needed for some highly specialized tasks, I have generally had disdain for consultants. Typically, they simply have not had enough skin in the game. Where past consultants could espouse opinions on what should be done, if the business failed as a partial consequence of bad advice, the consultant simply moved to a new client. In the age of autonomy where advances in tracking tools score the success and failure of each sole proprietor, amalgamated toward an objective accomplishment, failure will be transparent and known within the affected industry.

Tracking tools, i.e., controls have long been critical in effectively managing businesses. Keeping a pulse on all critical health factors in your business will continue to be important. New controls that monitor new configurations in business should provide opportunities for the creators of such tools. When business writers suggest that tightly controlled growth, things like the "20 mile per day march" are important for success, I say baloney. Demand is constant in very few industries. While people may always want and need to travel, buy food, buy insurance and many other things, they do not need to buy Nike shoes. They do not need to buy wood venetian blinds. They do not need many products and services which are elective. So, if you happen to run one of those companies, when demand heats up, you should be ready to grow quickly and grow profitably. Accelerated growth can cause major problems with financing, development and acquisition of capital items, development of talent and so on. That should not be a constraint; the ability to grow exponentially while in control is what your customers want. Drucker would say that anything that is not measured is ignored. Anything that is ignored may bite you. The frenzied concern for all facets of the business is critical.

At Eastbay, Rick Gering and Art Juedes had grown in every year of their existence; even in the year Nike had stripped away their right to sell Air products. When we joined forces, we installed rather rigid disciplines where daily indicators told us how we were performing, a business pulse. Monthly schedules were rigid with income statements and balance sheets completed by the tenth working day of the new month. Review meetings where someone owned and defended every line on the income statement were a must each month.

The attention to detailed controls produced a higher intensity. Soon, results allowed us to dump our existing bank where rates were charged at Prime plus 1% to a new lender who charged us LIBOR plus ½%.

In the five years leading up to our IPO, sales grew at 37% compounded annually but, profit grew at 43%. The key is to point out that you can grow fast and profitably.

It always seemed to me that the best way to think of business and life was not in cycles but as a pyramid. There is less likelihood that a business will grow, decline and rebuild than that it will grow, mature and die, just like the human body. Certainly, there are businesses like Southwest Airlines, Progressive Insurance, Intel and the like who perform well for decades. However, it is more likely that the frenzy needed to perform over decades will wane with aging of the people charged with running the business. So, rather than despair over the downside prospects demise, my philosophy is you make hay when the sun shines. You operate with the highest sense of controlled growth you can develop.

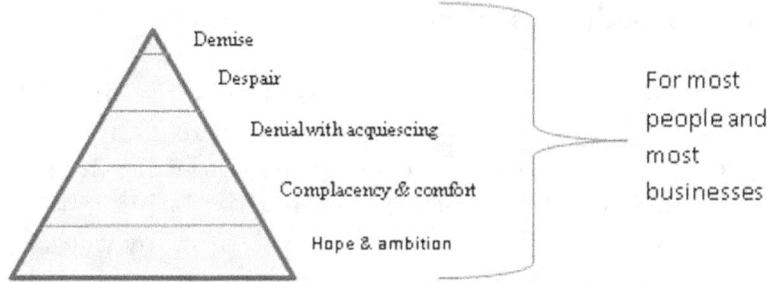

Like Maslow's labels for human needs, life and business are most often a pyramid. The only reason for not inverting the pyramid is the promise of something after life! Rebirth in business is possible. Rebirth in life is not possible but, regeneration can occur with attitude and the discipline to achieve results. In business, if you run like crazy for what you deem or perceive to be 60% of it life, you may have returned handsome results for the people who took the risk to fund the venture.

If you are in one of those rare ventures which sustains and even experiences rebirth, the frenzied route to rapid growth should not have hurt you if your attention to detail remained maniacal. The approach to life and business is always enhanced when we choose humor over anger at the prospect of our likely ultimate demise. Humor in life is the difference between what we deem lovable old people and cantankerous complaining old curmudgeons. And referring to the attitude you bring to work, there are many considerations.

My attitude long before reading "In Search of Excellence" was that I needed to communicate to everyone in the business that which we thought would be happening. Even if we were deciding to do nothing, it was a decision and it needed to be shared with all stakeholders. Having begun my work life as a janitor in an elementary school, I always hoped that I looked at each and every person in the businesses as a worthy team member.

With that said, my attitude was not based on some simplistic view of the world; it was calculated to keep our team more connected than many of our competitors who were deemed to be cold mannered and secretive. The calculating nature went to an extreme with a plant employee of many years named Art. Art was a kindly old fellow with arthritis that had nearly crippled him over the years of standing on a concrete floor at his punch press station. By age 60, Art was so slow as to effect production flow on numerous custom fabrication projects. When talk of forcing Art into disability occurred, the plant manager at that facility asked a few of us to discuss our options. The operations manager was a guy with a big heart and when we agreed to involve Art in discussions, rather than dictate to him, Art was thrilled. It turned out that Art simply did not want to spend 7 days a week at home with his wife. When we created a position where Art could wander the plant 3 shifts a week, moving papers rather than operating a huge press, he was happy. We promised him full pay and health insurance to age 65. When asked by one young new plant worker how we could be so kind my comments were simple. I told the young man I had worked six years in the same plant as Art. If we mistreated Art, would this young man, at age 18, want to risk the next 40 years on us only to be tossed out when he might be in no condition to work hard enough but still too young to retire. No, we wanted this young man's loyalty, commitment, hard work and ingenuity and for that, we had to pay a price.

You should not construe this to be kindness nor should it be considered manipulation. It is rather circumstance.

What do I believe to be true about the role of an executive? Within the role, it is helpful to stay personally removed from the implications of most issues and most personalities. It is in fact a job, not a life unto itself. The fine line between your head and your heart is sometimes hard to see, but, it should not be easy.

To perform consistently, balance between three executive prospective functions should be considered (and balance may not lead to equal weighty, merely appropriate weighting.) Operating skills, leadership and management are separate. They should stay separate in your consideration. There is an ever-present dichotomy between the desire to be benevolent and the need to be harsh. The key seems to me to be consistent fairness and honesty.

There is also the issue of integrity which gets bandied about by most retired executives as an integral part of success. When the word comes up, I have long since suggested that total integrity is great, once you can afford it. Before you reach a stage where complete integrity is used as your absolute filter, you should trust your instincts. If you have reached the rank of CEO, chances are that your instincts contain better criteria than you think. Before I engage my decision making, I do ask many questions. My ideas grow from discussions with others. Unlike my friend Atedo, I do learn when I speak. You should gauge how you learn best. But, more on how you learn will be discussed in the summary. I have always wanted others to see my contributions as valuable. In my early career, I would assert much about which I was uncertain. I always managed to assert the uncertain with great certainty. Only with the value of experience, especially failed experience did I gain the knowledge needed to be right more often than wrong. Coincidentally, with that knowledge came less need to be assertive.

At the risk of stating the obvious redundantly, qualifying questions should be asked:

- What is the task?
- What are we trying to accomplish?
- Why do it at all?

- What do we pay for it?
- What value is the job supposed to add?
- Have we engineered a disciplined process?

These are questions straight out of Dr. Ducker's suggestions. Until someone finds a better route for qualifying the information than may be available, this is a good discipline. Usually, if the questioning process is done properly, you will not need to use your gut to decide, those affected will know enough to buy into a path that their input helped create. And again, there need be no secrets about where you are and where you intend to go.

You can tell most people all you know and what you will do and they cannot gain advantage. The requirement to combine and balance the appropriate levels of leadership, operating skills and management are too subtle and too complex to allow most imitators to turn knowledge into results.

Knowledge is more easily attainable then at any point in history. Reducing knowledge to work, monitoring results, and maintaining performance will continue to be the exception rather than the rule. Winners continue working and winning. "Also-rans" continue to use new found knowledge as the basis for new dreams, with real results highly unlikely.

As a manager, I always loved my role, not just liked it, I loved it. I avoided any sense of jealousy in perspective. Jealously is a silly admission of defeat. Goals and work should be mental fillers if any jealous feelings arise. Knowledge, curiosity and work are rewarding simply in the doing.

Embrace your people but, do not envelope them. My best experiences were in companies where we had fewer than 100 people. You can know the names and something about 100 people. You cannot do the same with 1000 people. In the Age of Autonomy, developing as small a circle of contributors as you need to complete the tasks may be the best way to develop personal relationships that foster bonds that can be valuable to all in the future.

In more traditional business settings, I suggest that you want a family feel, but, they are not really your family or your people. They appropriately consider self-improvement opportunities at a higher level than you may know. In memorable fashion I have had a couple of instances when my key report has suggested that my contributions no longer justified my position. In both cases I was surprised and saddened. In one case the view was justified. The most important takeaway is that no matter how strong the link, no matter how successful the association, we are all just people. The better we understand, appreciate and calculate where relationships may go, the better prepared we will be to maximize opportunities. Frenzy for how human relations work, fit and contribution is critical.

With all that is required, it is important to genuinely have fun and stay calm. Although I have had a fair amount of success, I am still more apt to think of myself as a waiter than a diner. By recognizing the likelihood of failure, you can relax with occasional success.

There was terrific excitement in being allowed to run businesses from age 26 to 48. When I consider why I retired too young, the perspective is simple. I guess I don't care to be graded anymore. I care deeply about the ability to reason. Each discovery causes me to wonder about implications and possibilities. Few thoughts are novel, but, they are novel to me.

I also think that I know that if I worked, I would need to work with 100% effort, completely immersed. In any job assigned I found myself in love with my role. Construction, interior design, athletics and even the internet's first boom all seemed special and I felt privileged to be involved. Falling in love again post-60 might just be too much to expect in a life that is certainly well past the middle!

Summary

If the migration to autonomy creates the next new reality, what will we experience in threats and opportunities? Which functions, which programs will change, be eliminated or be created? How will workers relate to their employers and fellow workers? Who is likely to win and who is likely to lose?

Today, there is still an enormous cost associated with management. With autonomy much of this cost will go away. When we consider the management tasks of recruit, select, train, monitor and motivate, for the "company" most of these tasks will disappear. In autonomy, the sole proprietors (SP) will train themselves and sell their own skills. The SP will stay motivated by competing in an eat what you kill world. It is worth repeating again and again, these changes will not occur overnight, but, they will occur.

As suggested earlier, currency is one of the silly costs societies will legislate out of existence. Currencies differentiate areas and countries but, currency also travels free from view. Illegal aliens are compensated and drug dealers flourish. Taxes are easily evaded with "black market" exchanges of labor for cash. I remember asking a business group in Malmo, Sweden how in the world they could stay motivated to work when the tax rates equaled near 70%. That occurred more than 30 years ago and I will always remember the answers. They said don't be silly, 25% of our economy occurs in a black market where we all exchange cash for goods and services. In effect their widely criticized tax rate was not far from our U.S. rates.

So, in a world where paychecks are deposited automatically, where payments are deducted automatically and activity is reconciled online, we certainly do not need cash? Mobile devices already allow us to swipe payments. Transparency should create an opportunity to legislate equitable tax contributions by many more participants. Something like the flat tax Peter Drucker long supported might finally gain legs. While this automation and illumination would wipe out a substantial function in banking, it will nonetheless be effective.

Further, beyond private sector change, governments should change dramatically in the age of autonomy. If governments exist to serve the people, people should ask how services can be most responsive and least costly.

When you consider the mobilizing capacity of social networking seen recently in the Middle East, it is easy to appreciate how effective collective action can be if harnessed properly.

In history, the most dramatic change based on how information affected the world occurred with the reformation. While protests against the church had long been registered, there was no way to coordinate or organize the protest. Then, Guttenberg developed the printing press and Martin Luther could post protests quickly and broadly and drastic changes occurred where a Protestant ethic changed the world of work and religion.

Today, the ability to act by referendum should, by implication, eliminate an entire sector of government in the U.S. Local governments are needed in order to respond to day to day needs. Trash removal, street cleaning and the like on the low tech end along with education and safety on the upper end should be local. It is hard to imagine national armies maintaining police and fire safety when dispersed from central control. While education will likely advance most dramatically with online tools such as Khan Academy, social implications seem best enhanced when real touch is associated with advancing technology.

On a national level, things like transportation and defense are best managed from a central location. One can debate centralized management of health and social services but, it is unlikely they will disappear via referendum.

State governments, all 50 of them, seem to me to be unnecessary. With education dominated locally and by boards of regents, budgets are mechanical and can easily be handled on a centralized basis. Transportation administrative expenses are duplicated at national and state levels. The duplication of executive, legislative and judicial functions is not only in duplicate, it is also often in conflict. Allowances and limits for most things in a knowledge based world should be the same no matter which location we live. Silly competitions for business often result in wasteful spending by competing states.

Eliminating government bodies does not mean centralize into impervious hierarchical functions. Conversely, it means decentralize with information for all to see. It means votes can occur immediately on most issues. Change can occur quickly. Certainly, to avoid pure democracy which might be akin to anarchy, new rules and newly empowered referees would need to be considered. For any such change to occur, movement from the bottom up would be essential. State politicians and administrative associates are not likely to push to put themselves out of work.

There are volumes written about the decline in religious participation throughout the world with the exception of sub-Saharan Africa. The success of religions seems to me to be enhanced when uncertainty exists. When we don't know what will happen, faith can help us endure, accept and find hope. When terrible things do happen, faith may provide the only comfort that keeps us from total despair. Even though restrictions and sacrifices are required as prices to be paid for religions, there has been satisfaction in accommodating such sacrifices. With vast increases in knowledge continuing at an ever increasing pace, uncertainty will likely continue to decline. Where religious scholars understood the contradictions in the history of religions, today, history, current events and behavior concerns are available for all to view. If this knowledge in the Age of Autonomy advances, the negative implications of religion will decline but, so too will the positive benefits.

Back to the business of business; as suggested at the beginning of this summary, there will be great change associated with an Age of Autonomy. A threat may be the loss of valuable mental health associated with the interaction of associates working for a company. It is likely that in an eat what you kill world, an even faster work pace will preclude the lounge around time in break rooms and around the water cooler. Balancing the loss of this social benefit is the sense of self-reliance that should foster various emotions and actions ranging from aggressiveness, competitiveness, innovative thinking, fraternity building, satisfaction and more.

The more autonomous functions become, the more executives will need tools which provide the data base for who does what, where they are located, what is their availability, what will it cost, with whom have they worked, what are past successes? Building scores and maintaining such information will be an area of opportunity not unlike the business rating firms we have seen for decades.

Change in the past created excitement and fear. Fear is typically heightened when we did not know what was around the next corner. Would we encounter a pathway or a blockade? In this knowledge age, what we are able to see is exponentially clearer than was seen in the past. In a world where such great availability of knowledge is at hand, creating harmony will be the new world of the executive in business. Complete knowledge completely frees those who attain it. But, the productivity of knowledge still requires work. The tools needed to make work effective should create great opportunities for the innovative entrepreneur who is willing to take risk and to work. The speed with which businesses can safely grow grows proportionately with controls available to gauge business health factors.

As mechanical advances have fostered the general availability of knowledge, champions who perform with constant frenzy will still be needed. The various traits obvious in various CEO's will still exist at a premium. The "monomaniac on a mission" Dr. Drucker described as entrepreneurial is likely the new CEO. Knowledge and knowledge related tools should make the new CEO a specialist, a generalist, a psychologist, a conductor, an analyst and a financier. The new tool makers will build facilitation tools!

Creative destruction should take on a new meaning with the Age of Autonomy. Adam Smith's "invisible hand" should be transparent and more obvious to all in the Age of Autonomy. When capitalist naysayers scorn the excesses of greed tied to Adam Smith's free market support, they forget to mention that Adam Smith was the Professor of Moral Philosophy at the University of Glasgow. Adam Smith's "Theory of Moral Sentiments" preceded "Wealth of Nations" by seventeen years. It is interesting that in the earlier work, Smith suggests that the individual must scrutinize his own morals and behaviors as he would someone else's. In the Age of Autonomy, this self-audit would seem appropriate when competing one on one rather than simply as part of a company.

When Karl Marx wrote about Creative Destruction, he wrote as a response to over-production through the destruction of capital which resulted in barbaric treatment of the masses. For Marx, capitalism led to dominance and danger from those controlling wealth.

For Joseph Schumpeter a century later, Creative Destruction came to be defined as the effectiveness of capital. The forces of capitalism assured that what existed will be replaced by something better.

In the Age of Autonomy, Creative Destruction will be the intellectual capital which erases old norms and sets new standards. It will increasingly migrate toward the elimination of administration and specialization. Capital will slowly become the Private Property of the Mind. My mind is my house. Its contents are under my control. You may visit me and I may visit you, but, you do not control the supply of that which feeds me nor me you. Tyranny in any form cannot survive where fear of the unknown is no longer a factor. The enhancement of self-rule in autonomy should create a higher sense of reward no matter the task.

Management, the process of moving things or people toward the creation and production of a product or service, physically or by delegation will still exist in the Age of Autonomy. It will be better.

While we discuss "final frontiers," in fact, the new frontiers look very much like the old frontiers. Frontiersmen searched for the means to achieve independence. Conversely, the means we have developed have fostered independence. Now, more and more, we each rely on ourselves for the production which provides survival and prosperity. The loss of security within community is a threat. However, if we embrace leadership in individual self-reliance, we may also maintain and enhance the "Yankee ingenuity" that has been the basis for creativity and entrepreneurism beyond any nation in history.

Not unlike risk in any age, individuals in the Age of Autonomy will vary in their sense of excitement or fear over the risks related to change.

There has never been a lack of imagination related to how knowledge can be applied to create or change products and services. Fear of failure and/or the simple lack of initiative needed to reduce ideas to work prevent most people from acting on their visions. On the other hand, some people feel exhilaration over the mere prospect of risk.

Years ago I was asked to list some of the traits I thought applied to people who succeed. People who succeed learn to image success. They spend much of their free time dreaming about how they will look in the role that they hope to have for themselves. Good actors project themselves into their roles, project yourself into your future, image the successes that you plan to attain. See yourself taking the first steps.

People who succeed find a fit. There is a personality test which now has been validated to the point of near total acceptability in the psychology field. The test says that, taking for granted that you are a sane person, you may be an administrative type, field general type, an architect type, and the list goes on and on. It is important to recognize that each of these 16 types fit better with some types than with others. When I suggest that people who succeed find a fit, I suggest that there is an organization or a place whose culture is right or at least more apt to be right for every individual. There are usually no "wrong people", only wrong roles or wrong relationships.

People who succeed manage their buckets. Each of us has a gauge inside. Our buckets run from one to ten. When our buckets are filled beyond ten, something spills over and, that can be very ugly. People who succeed manage their stress levels by staying aware of what they are doing to themselves and what their environments are doing for them. We manage stress through an occasional, purposeful escape into our own fantasy world where we imagine things as better. We manage our bucket by physically not overusing those things which contribute to excessive stress. What happens when we ingest too much caffeine or too much nicotine or too much alcohol or engage in too little exercise is that our bucket, which goes to ten before it spills over, is consistently running at an unreasonable high level, let's say seven or eight. At that level, it takes far less to push us over the top than it would if we had not artificially increased our stress level by overuse. I'm suggesting that you plan enough exercise so that you allow your body to release the chemicals that our bodies do release in response to exercise. This in turn gives our buckets more room because, people who succeed do have problems and, success is better preserved through logical rather than stressful response to problems.

People who succeed play the game of life with intensity. They may change course now and then. It may seem as if what they are doing does not tie with their goal, but in fact, people who succeed keep their goal constantly in front of them. They know that life is "not a dress rehearsal".

People who succeed find opportunity in failure. Murphy's Law says that anything that can go wrong will, and it will happen at the most inopportune time. If you accept the fact that failure is bound to be part of your life, for only those doing nothing avoid failure, then it is important that you recognize that people who succeed truly do find opportunity in failure. Avoid being indignant in failure and avoid puffery in success. I don't remember the last time that I truly analyzed success. Success is something that we bask in. Success is something that we enjoy, but it is not something that we analyze. On the other hand, I also can't remember a time when having failed, I have not spent countless hours analyzing what I did that caused failure. With the analysis comes an education, an education that's paid for with countless hours and a high degree of stress. People who succeed can build on their successes, even if they never succeed in figuring out what it was they did right. But, people who succeed also capitalize on their failures by selling the probability of their future success, based on the knowledge they have gained.

People who succeed know what luck is. Luck isn't being in the right place at the right time and as a result, enjoying great success. Luck is being in the right place at the right time with the willingness to take risk, personally, in an effort to succeed. The lucky lottery winner put up the cash. The lucky business success put up the cash and/or risked the career.

People who succeed do something. The greatest failure of all is the failure that occurs when you do nothing. Doing something means that you look for solutions not scapegoats. Doing something means that you try to know all of the facts, listing what you think you should do and then following your list until you accomplish what needs to be done. When you do something, even if you fail, you will learn. Also, in many instances, people have done something and although it wasn't the right thing, they have stumbled onto even greater opportunity simply from having acted.

People who succeed depend on themselves. They depend on their own talents, not just favorable conditions. They don't share the losers' excessive vulnerability to the opinion of others. That is not to say that people who succeed do not have heroes. People who succeed identify the strengths in their heroes or mentors that they hope to imitate.

People who succeed see the need to balance the hard work that is required today with the planning necessary for success tomorrow. Peter Drucker suggested that we should keep one eye on the mountain and one eye on the grindstone. Hard work alone, without planning, results in the need to work harder than necessary each day because you have never taken the time to think about what the future might bring, nor prepared yourself with the proper tools, physical or mental. On the other hand, an imbalance where too much time is spent on planning obviously results in failure to complete the work required today.

People who succeed know how they learn best. They sense the "aha" that tells them that they are in their best zone. They focus on scheduling their lives to maximize their use of time. When I referred to an "aha" moment regarding Atedo in the Influencer's Chapter, it was the genesis for considering how we learn. It seems to me that there are degrees of learning which occur at different levels for each person. Since it has not been based on study, I can only offer my perspective. Because we are exposed to each of the routes to learning, the "aha" sense must come from within. The routes to learning include:

1. Observing and analyzing
2. Listening
3. Reading and studying
4. Interacting
5. Writing
6. Teaching

There may be routes I have missed. I offer the list so you can consider which causes the greatest "aha" moment for you. My sense is that the degrees of effectiveness vary wildly with each of us. After considering Atedo's assertion that he only learned when he listened, I began to think about how I learned best.

It seemed to me that reading fired my brains connectors. Writing had long been a struggle for me. I sensed that I rambled with little ability to be concise. Teaching or giving speeches always made me self-conscious, concerned for how I looked, how I sounded and how I had prepared. I sensed that I was quite observant of others and qualified to assess how people felt and how they thought. My listening skills needed honing as I found myself more anxious to talk than to listen. But then, while leading a group in a strategy setting session, I felt that "aha". Clearly, asking questions, listening to input from others, considering implications and suggesting optional routes for actions was the firing activity that caused my brain to feel that this was my best route to learn and to contribute.

As you move toward an autonomous contributor phase, it will be important for you to keep your sensors acutely aware of how your brain fires best. This is not to say that any single route is the only route, it is simply the best route. While I must still read, listen, write, speak/teach and observe, the best use of my brain will be by interacting. Even as you seek and find your best route to learn and thereby contribute and achieve, you will likely need to try many options to hit your optimum route to success. Consider if you will that most entrepreneurial ventures fail or succeed in something entirely different than planned. As individuals' trend more and more toward singular contribution, finding to best product, the best service and/or the best people with whom to connect will necessarily be by trial and error. The individual will need to be patient and persevere. It will be like Edison's perspective in his quote about failure, "I have not failed, I've just found 10,000 ways that will not work." Once you find the route that does work for you, autonomous contribution should provide a multi-faceted sense of reward absent for most individuals for over a century.

When I alluded early on to farmers and blacksmiths as autonomous contributors, it did not escape me that serfs and servants did abound throughout history. As we migrate toward autonomy, classes of contribution will still exist, autonomy will go to those who consider, who plan and who work! In the past, successful output relied on the association and performance of a large group of people. In the Age of Autonomy, smaller groups with more intimate awareness of how others in their fraternity perform will be an important key to success.

People who succeed see change as filled with opportunities, not threats. The sense that curiosity, conclusion and work will lead to success is compelling for people who succeed.

There is a very old saying, "the longest journey begins with a single step." The saying says nothing about how onerous the first step can be for almost everyone.

If a migration toward autonomy moves at the rapid pace that it likely will move, it will truly be unsettling for most people. The sense that we are drifting that has dominated the 21st century may meet a new reality where people begin to broadly recognize that we will never return to full employment through integrated operations where people felt comforted by connection even though they may not have been satisfied by their positions.

That "first step" is almost always a mental hurdle for many of the reasons already mentioned. Fears of failure, complacency, comfort with mediocrity, etc., all make approaching the first step all the more difficult. Once we take the initiative to take the first step, the next step is almost always less difficult. Certainly, there will be more hurdles, but, having dealt with the first hurdle, the start, subsequent hurdles seem less threatening. You gain the confidence that accompanies success. You are a winner based on the fact that you generated the energy to begin. And, somehow, someway, winners keep winning.

So, get started. Look at the implications of autonomy as it relates to all of business and business functions. It will be a very exciting time to work.

Epilogue

As I scribbled notes for years, my thought was always that some benefit might accrue to you, my sons. As I finished this effort, I reflected on my own father's life and what it meant to me. While his living was made as a furnace repair man, his army years in World War II had a great impact on how he lived. He never spoke of the war except to say he served in Burma, had contracted malaria and had seen many people die. In the final days of his life, as he lay dying in our family living room, I asked for the details of his life so I could write them down. When he told my mother what I was doing, I sensed a keen appreciation in his tone, as if I was adding purpose to his existence. That appreciation caused me to wonder what disciplines a person needs in order to live like you are already gone. Like most successful regimens, it seems to me that what is required is in fact, discipline. The word itself is telling; Disciple, a follower. Line a course of action or a long thin mark on a surface. For a life to feel full, happy and productive it seems that disciplined work toward goals is critical.

While the final two influencers I want to write a note about were not business people, they each nonetheless have had an influence on how I think and act. One was my first co-worker and the other, a friend met after I retired. At 14, my first regular job was as a janitor's helper in a Catholic grade school. My fellow worker was Mike Hartl, an 84 year old retired farmer. He was a 4'11" retired farmer who had migrated to America in 1905 only to return to his Prussian homeland to fight in World War I. He eventually returned to the U.S. and farmed until age 80. When I asked Mike why he was still working at age 84, he said that his young bride no longer appreciated his energy level and he needed to work it off. She was 69 years old and while I thought I knew what he meant, I didn't ask. After two years together, I found factory work and we lost touch for 10 years. At 26, with a bit more freedom in my schedule as a company head, I started to visit Mike for one hour each week. He was 96 and still anxious to discuss world events over a beer. When I asked him how it was that at his age, unlike all the other elderly people I knew, he never complained about aches and pains. Mike said that he had the same aches and pain as all elderly people; he just chose not to talk about them. In broken English, he said, "Harry, if I talk about the pain of an old man, you will not be excited to see me. If I tell you about old world events as you tell me about the new world, we will stay friends." Mike lived 4 more years to 100 and I have never forgotten his message.

When I retired to "Snowbird" status in South Beach I continued to run for exercise but in sporadic fashion. Years later, while sitting on the beach, a local running celebrity known simply as the Raven asked people to join him for his 100,000 mile run on March 29, 2009. I had heard of Raven but thought he ran slowly and I was unaware of the distance he ran. Well, it turned out that Raven ran 8 miles every day and had not missed a day since January 1, 1975. When asked how he could run through hurricanes, concussions, sickness and all of life's other challenges, Raven simply said that he needed to maintain discipline. Can you name anyone who, despite health, family, weather and work would show up at the same place every day for 14,000 days in a row to run 8 miles in the sand? Since my first run with Raven, I have joined him 400 times and it has been an honor and with awe. More than 1600 people have joined Raven at the 5th Street Lifeguard station to complete the 8 mile run. While many only run once, the numbers vary up to 1500 times for Gringo, the closest to Raven in total.

Finally, with what started as a short journal, I am satisfied that I have left some mark for you, my sons. I challenge you to be curious, to create, to change, to ignore most rules which are only fabricated limits, to discipline yourself with a willingness to start and a confidence to persevere. After all, long before there was a t-shirt company, I was known for saying the same thing in response to many questions…Life is Good!

www.ingramcontent.com/pod-product-compliance
Lightning Source LLC
Chambersburg PA
CBHW072025190526

45166CB00015B/500